RECLA[IMING]

AUTHENTIC

FUNDA-
MENTALISM

By Douglas R. McLachlan

Highway 55 at 900 Forestview Lane North
Plymouth, Minnesota 55441-5934
phone 1.800.827.1043 or 763.417.8250
email info@centralseminary.edu
web www.centralseminary.edu

Central Baptist
SEMINARY

Reclaiming Authentic Fundamentalism
by Douglas R. McLachlan

©2002 Dr. Douglas R. McLachlan
Central Baptist Seminary
Highway 55 at 900 Forestview Lane North
Plymouth, Minnesota 55441-5934

ISBN 0-918407-02-8

Printed in the United States of America

ACKNOWLEDGEMENTS

I wish to thank Dr. Les Ollila, whose life and message provided many of the seminal thoughts for this book. It was Les that God used to provide healing and a haven in a time of hurt, and to give foundational direction in this project.

Also, I want to thank Mrs. Kelly Filipiak, who served as my secretary during the composition of this manuscript and who worked tirelessly and efficiently to put it into the computer.

Special thanks are due to Dr. Carl Herbster, Mr. Craig Krueger and other members of the AACS staff for their encouragement, expertise, and help in the matters of editing and publishing. Carl's ministry is in many ways a model of that to which we aspire in this book. Jan and Debbie designed and finished the cover art and Craig's expertise in grammar and expression has proven invaluable.

I am grateful to Calvary Baptist Theological Seminary of Lansdale, Pennsylvania for permission to include materials printed in the *Calvary Baptist Theological Journal.*

I feel a special indebtedness to authors and speakers I cannot name. Every person is a composite of the people who have influenced him. Some statements in this book are sourced in others who over the years have impacted my life. Unfortunately, I have long since forgotten the precise source and, therefore, I am unable to give proper credit. I apologize ahead of time for this and am prepared to make it right whenever I am informed by such sources.

I appreciate the help of my colleague at Northland, Mr. Doug Bennett, who was willing to read the manuscript chapter by chapter and make helpful suggestions. Thanks, too, to Pastors John K. Hutcheson, Norm Pyle, and John Vaughn who read the entire manuscript, made valuable suggestions and encouraged me in the project.

Finally, a special note of appreciation is due my wife, Marie, who has always been my strongest supporter in every ministry task we have undertaken, including this one.

DEDICATION

To the next generation of fundamentalists:
May you live authentically
in the Church
and minister redemptively
to the world.

FOREWORD

When some hear the word **Fundamentalist**, their minds conjure up a variety of images. Unfortunately, these mental pictures do not always reflect Biblical thinking and sometimes the images are of radical, power-hungry, anti-God world dictators who exploit their people and abuse their culture. There are those, even in Christian circles, who have mockingly said that a fundamentalist is one who has a lot of **fun** and a lot of **dam** but very little **mental**. Sadly, some in the fundamentalist movement have tragically provided enough observable data to fuel those views.

While this mislabeling of fundamentalism is grossly inaccurate, there do clearly appear to be two spectrums within conservative Christianity with a lot of other mixed philosophies in between. On one side of the spectrum **apologetics** is magnified and leadership does a commendable job of expositing Scripture, but often they cower from issues and ignore controversies. Separation, whether personal or ecclesiastical, is considered legalism or pharisaism and is a non-issue. The other side of this spectrum magnifies **polemics**, which is an attack on another's position. These leaders typically focus on attacking error or perceived error and sometimes are irresponsible in handling the Word of God accurately or honestly. Separation, on this side of the spectrum, becomes the main focus, and there seems to be an absence of joy, a conditional love, and a lack of freedom in their Christian walk. The "free" thinker sees the fundamentalist as though he were in bondage to the law, knowing nothing of freedom in grace. The fundamentalists, on the other hand, think that the opposing spectrum ignores seeing God in all of His attributes and forgets that grace teaches us to deny

v

"ungodliness and worldly lusts" and to "live soberly, righteously, and godly, in this present world." Consequently, the cause of Christ continues to suffer through a lack of balance between these views and there is a proud refusal to admit the error by both sides. When Nehemiah's men built the walls, the builders had a sword in one hand and a trowel in the other. Battling while you are building seems to be the balance.

The foundational philosophy of a ministry has always had an effect on the superstructure of that ministry. There is a dangerous trend in ministries today to overlook the foundation of doctrine to speed up the building of the superstructure. When a doctrinal foundation is overlooked for a focus on growth, pragmatism becomes the controlling philosophy. Ministries move from theism to practical atheism through the vehicle of pragmatism. The problem with pragamatism is that it does work. However, a greater consequence is that a ministry's dependence on God wanes, resulting in a loss of God's presence and a compromise of truth. Let us remember that some pragmatic ideas to build the superstructure may be logical but not theological.

This excellent work by Dr. McLachlan comes out of a heart burdened by the dangers of the extremes. He has attempted to show a Biblical philosophy of ministry while issuing a call for an authentic, Biblical balance that is reflected in both growth and obedience, holiness, and grace. I believe that you will find this book a breath of fresh air in the maze of confusion that exists. I pray that you will be challenged to honestly establish a strong Biblical ministry with a holy foundation and construct a superstucture that is built not only with results in mind but also by means which give a proper opinion of the character of God. If you will approach this work as a leader with an open mind and an open heart, you cannot help but be challenged to have an authentic ministry as well as a balanced life.

Dr. Les Ollila, Northland Baptist Bible College

vi

PREFACE

The newest generational phenomenon in this country is the generation which has been dubbed the "baby busters." Born between 1965 and 1983, there are 68 million of them and they are inheriting a world which desperately needs fixing. "They are ennobled by a sense that they are a Repair Generation who will make the world better, but embittered by a belief that" others before them should have started this process and those after them will be the ones benefitted by their efforts. As one of their spokesmen put it: "We feel like a generation of janitors"[1].

In some ways, this is how I visualize the emerging generation of young fundamentalists. They are inheriting an ecclesiastical world which needs fixing. My generation has managed to leave more than a little litter on the theological landscape, and like their generational counterparts in the secular realm, I am praying that this new generation of fundamentalists will become a repair generation too. However, quite unlike their secular counterparts,the emerging generation of fundamentalists must never be embittered by the rebuilding process, only ennobled. There is something intrinsically rewarding and fulfilling attached to rebuilding, even if it is primarily for others and not for ourselves.

Our purpose in this book is to define some of what has gone wrong in Fundamentalism and, at least in part, prescribe a solution; to demonstrate why a rebuilding is necessary and bring into focus some of the areas where it must take place. In doing this, it is important for the reader to know that we operate from a specific set of presuppositions:

1.   Our critique is a self-critique; we ourselves are fundamentalists and are deeply committed to Biblical Fundamentalism.

vii

2. Our approach is neither a reaction to nor a rebellion against Fundamentalism. It is an appeal for revival within it.

3. Our goal is to be constructive, not destructive. We have no desire to join the ranks of those who find some form of delight or acceptance by engaging in fundamentalist bashing.

4. Our strategy is to be transparent and honest about our problems rather than masking, disguising, camouflaging, or even denying that we have them.

5. Our perspective is not "Rehoboamic" (I Kings 12:1-17). In the history of Israel it was Rehoboam who repudiated the counsel of the elders and embraced exclusively the counsel of the young. We believe it is essential to recognize the accomplishments of the past and to appreciate not only the lessons we learn, but the blessing we inherit from it. It is in vogue in our existentialist age to be contemptuous of and sometimes combative toward our history. The result of such a negative focus toward our historic past might be the tragic loss of a meaningful future. We wish to affirm our respect for founding fathers.

6. Our spirit is not one of being the "knowers," as though we are a new breed of gnostics. We are trying to be the learners, seeking to discern what is wrong and struggling to discover what can be done to make it right.

So we begin our task by defining the hindrances to a balanced Fundamentalism and identifying those ingredients which have prohibited authenticity in its super-structure. Following that we continue with a discussion of four key areas of ministry, which, if understood properly and fleshed out biblically, could enable us to take a giant step toward reclaiming an authentic variety of Fundamentalism. These areas have to do with servant leadership, urgent evangelism, expository preaching, and Christian separation. Finally, we close with a call for Biblical revival, the ultimate solution to the ills which face any community of believers in Jesus Christ.

Martin E. Marty and R. Scott Appleby, who have given direction to the *Fundamentalism Project*, would like us to think that Fundamentalism is simply a reaction to modernity by people who prefer to live by the standards of antiquity. But this is not so! The belief system of contemporary Fundamentalism is not sourced in its reaction to the cultural milieu, but in its understanding of the Biblical mandate. Fundamentalists hold to a set of beliefs which transcend all cultures and all times because those beliefs are sourced in the eternal Word of God. And when our *behavioral patterns* begin to match with our *belief system*, Fundamentalism will once again become the effective agent of redemptive change which God has always intended for it to be. To this end these words have been written.

CONTENTS

Contents	Page

Chapter One

Hindrances to a Balanced Fundamentalism — 1

Chapter Two

Identifying True Leadership — 23

Chapter Three

Rediscovering Authentic Evangelism — 54

Chapter Four

Practicing Authentic Proclamation — 89

Chapter Five

Implementing Authentic Separation — 115

Chapter Six

Recovering Our Spiritual Vitality — 144

Footnotes — 158

Bibliography — 163

CHAPTER ONE

HINDRANCES TO A BALANCED FUNDAMENTALISM

"Failure to express holiness and love simultaneously turns God's people and God's servants into eccentric caricatures instead of authentic pictures of the Christ we represent."

"'No, don't dig up the past! Dwell on the past and you'll lose an eye!' But the proverb goes on to say: 'Forget the past and you'll lose both eyes'" (Aleksandr Solzhenitsyn).

Kirsopp Lake, a noted theological liberal, when describing Fundamentalism wrote these words:

> It is a mistake, often made by educated persons who happen to have but little knowledge of historical theology, to suppose that Fundamentalism is a new and strange form of thought. It is nothing of the kind: it is the . . . survival of a theology which was once universally held by all Christians . . . . The Fundamentalist may be wrong; I think that he is. But it is we who have departed from the tradition, not he, and I am sorry for the fate of anyone who tries to argue with a Fundamentalist on the basis of authority. The Bible and the *corpus theologicum* of the Church is on the Fundamentalist side.[1]

It is no surprise, therefore, that for generations there have been many who were committed to what is commonly called Fundamentalism. It is because of the *integrity* of the *foundation*, the innate rightness of its principal tenets. Whatever the faults of Fundamentalism, there is a foundation undergirding her which cannot be matched by any other theological movement.

Jesus made very clear the indispensable necessity of a proper foundation (Matthew 7:24-27). Our own human experience confirms this. None of us would be foolish enough to invest the financial resources which are necessary in our day to construct a building without first insisting that a proper foundation be laid. First we would see to it that deep footings and a sound foundation were put in place, and thereafter we would be prepared to make the necessary investments for the erection of the edifice. And if it is true that foundations are indispensable architecturally, it is equally true that they are indispensable theologically.

Notwithstanding, though the foundation of Fundamentalism "standeth sure," the superstructure is suspect. And the unique thing about a foundation is that it is hidden from view, while the superstructure is visible to all. Perhaps this accounts for the sense of disillusionment which seems to prevail among so many young fundamentalists. What they see and hear of Fundamentalism, with some obvious exceptions, is often disappointing to them. As one young correspondent recently wrote to me:

> It seems to me that if Fundamentalism claims to be the most doctrinally pure form of Christianity which is most worthy of God's blessing, then Fundamentalism as a movement should be demonstrably superior to other groups. Ethical standards for pastors should be higher, Fundamentalist preaching should be superior, Fundamentalist schools should have a stronger commitment to academic and spiritual excellence and

Fundamentalist churches should exemplify
the characteristics which made the early
church so potent. Either Fundamentalism
must move toward these ideals or it very
well could become another form of dead
orthodoxy.

So, on the one hand, second- and third-generation
Fundamentalists see the superstructure of Fundamentalism
as troubled and giving the appearance of disintegration;
while, on the other hand, they see the superstructure of
Neo-evangelicalism as triumphant and giving the
appearance of revitalization. While superficial
"appearances" are generally not reliable sources of "reality,"
nevertheless *the shock* of this realization can have a
stunning effect on young, idealistic thinkers who are hungry
for the kind of ministry which both glorifies God and
quenches and satisfies human thirst and hungers.

Perhaps those of us in the older generation should
face ourselves squarely here. It might be easy to excoriate
second- and third-generation Fundamentalists for their
audacity in asking certain of these questions, but it is
probably not wise. Instead we should be willing to listen
with sensitive attention and then respond with Biblical
precision. More than this, we must sense the *urgency* of
this confrontation and its implications to the next generation
of Fundamentalism if we fail to meet it sensitively and
Biblically.

Without a proper foundation, no movement can long
remain loyal to Jesus Christ. So the solution to our
problems within Fundamentalism is *not to abandon* a sound
foundation for a troubled one, *but to address* the issue of
rebuilding within Fundamentalism an authentic
superstructure in the place of one which is troubled. This

rebuilding represents a generational commitment. It is a task which will require discipline, devotion, and dedication. It will not be the way of easy going self-indulgence, nor will it attract those who are smitten with moral anemia. For such people, the possible results of rebuilding the superstructure of Fundamentalism are not worth the high cost. But for those who have confidence in the retrieving efficacy of divine grace, and who can visualize the dynamic potential of a revived Fundamentalism, whose foundation remains sound and whose superstructure becomes authentic, this intoxicating prospect becomes all the motivation they need to make whatever sacrifice is necessary to see it materialize.

In this chapter, we will be looking at the hindrances to a balanced Fundamentalism—the issues which have prohibited the movement from maintaining superstructural integrity.

Being Better Fighters than Builders

Fundamentalists have developed a reputation for exalting polemics over apologetics. *Polemics* comes from a Greek root meaning "to make war, to fight" and it is descriptive of armed conflict. *Apologetics* comes from a Greek root meaning "to defend" and carries the notion of a well-thought-through defense, the justification of an idea. This reputation means that we sometimes find it easier to attack another's point of view than to defend our own; that we are too often better known for caustic criticisms of perceived error than for careful defenses of revealed truth. But caustic criticisms are almost always counter-productive. They tend to push the undecided over the brink toward a less Biblical position. On the other hand, careful defenses are almost always constructively productive. They tend to lead the undecided away from the brink toward a more Biblical position.

It seems to me that we have lost more men to the cause of Fundamentalism because of the ugliness of our spirit rather than the content of our message, by our disposition rather than by our position. What is needed is a reversal of emphasis. It isn't that we should never engage in polemics. But like Nehemiah, we should first be known for our building and then for our fighting.

Essential Qualities

In I Timothy 3:3, Paul lays out three great qualities of spiritual leadership, which every fundamentalist who aspires to authenticity should take seriously.

First, Paul says that we should be *"no striker" (me plekten)*. It describes someone who is pugnacious and quick-tempered, someone who explodes with his fists and is anxious to exchange blows in the face of provocation. This is precisely what the godly man does not do. He never assaults others and neither is he a bully (II Timothy 2:24-26).

Second, he requires that we be *"patient" (epieikes)*. Matthew Arnold called it "sweet reasonableness." It is a portrait of mercifulness, yieldedness, and forgiveness which is gentle, unselfish, and patient. There is nothing so strong as gentleness and there is nothing so gentle as real strength (Matthew 11:28-30; II Corinthians 10:1). It describes the capacity for tempering justice with mercy, of refusing to insist upon one's rights, and of forgiving when one has a perfect right to condemn.

Joseph demonstrated this patience toward his brothers and toward Potiphar's wife when he finally had it in his power to avenge their wrongs. It was the spirit of David, who, when on two separate occasions he could have snuffed out the life of Saul, refused to touch *"the Lord's anointed."* And it was the spirit of Jesus, who, when He was reviled and beaten, refused to respond in kind, but instead uttered the burden of His heart for all humanity: *"Father, forgive them, for they know not what they do."* And this is a spirit which is desperately needed within our fundamentalist ranks and has too often been conspicuous by its absence. If it were more often present, a world of hostilities could be avoided.

Finally, Paul commands that God's men are not to be brawlers *(amachon)*. This idea exhorts God's people to be peaceable, tolerant, disinclined to fight. It pictures a spiritual leadership which is uncontentious. On the surface this is puzzling. Every serious student of Scripture knows that no man can embrace the Christian faith without integrating into his life a dimension of militancy. Authentic Christians are always prepared to defend the faith as Paul and others of the apostles did, and the refusal to do so on some bogus ground of feeble pacifism is the lowest form of false pietism. So what does Paul mean when he requires that we be peaceable, tolerant, and disinclined to fight? He means that God's man is never trigger-happy, offensively aggressive, or looking for a fight; that he never explodes with anger; and that he never views the battle as the first step in resolving a problem, but, as the last step, coming only after all other means have been carefully explored and fully exhausted.

However, when all such means have failed, and the preservation of truth is at stake, this peaceable man who is disinclined to fight, and is marked by a sweet reasonableness, is prepared to stand and to engage in the good fight, the noble battle which defends truth in a fallen world (II Timothy 4:7).

There is a valuable insight in this scenario. When a violent man fights, after a while no one really pays any attention because that is what he always does. But when a peaceable man fights, there is moral weight! It gains the attention of sensitive and perceptive observers because it is so uncharacteristic. The battle is perceived to be vital, and therefore, worthy of support.

Behaving Brazenly and Abrasively
rather than Boldly

Unfortunately, there has been a perception among some fundamentalists that one has not spoken either Biblically or boldly unless he has spoken meanly or harshly. But this is clearly contradicted by Scripture. In Ephesians 4:13-16 Paul deals with the theme of Christian maturity. At the very heart of this emphasis we find these words: *"speaking the truth in love"* (4:15). Actually, *aletheuontes* includes more than mere speech. If the English would allow it, it should be translated, "truthing in love." It demands that we honor the truth in what we are, say, and do; in disposition, dialogue, and deed. And Paul seems to be suggesting that there is no authentic honoring of truth unless it is expressed in a context of love. Love is not merely the accompaniment of truth, it is its atmosphere. These two great virtues, both of which are grounded in the very nature of God, are inextricably bound up with one another: "Truth becomes hard if it is not softened by love; love becomes soft if it is not strengthened by truth."[2] One of the supreme evidences of spiritual maturity is not only the proclamation of the right message—truth—but the projection of the right mood—love.

Boldness in Scripture never means harshness. The Greek word means, literally, "all speech, all words" and carries the connotation of telling the whole story. Biblically, boldness is genuineness or fullness of communication, the courage to tell the whole truth both comprehensively and compassionately. Practically, this means that Christians are not at liberty to water down the Gospel so that it is less objectionable, and therefore more palatable to the secular mind. We must tell the whole story, including the reality of sin and the necessity of repentance, sharing with people not only what Christ offers but also what Christ demands. The courage to do that is what the Bible calls boldness, and there is nothing in it which is incompatible with "speaking the truth in love."

Focusing on Mechanical Forms
rather than Biblical Principles

The first and clearest evidence that one has slipped into this mode of thought is the tendency to confuse traditional forms with Biblical substance. This problem is not new. Even Jesus was compelled to say: *"Full well ye reject* [set aside, cancel out, frustrate] *the commandment of God* [Biblical substance], *that ye may keep your own tradition* [traditional forms]" (Mark 7:9). In such a context there develops a *status quo* rigidity when it comes to the matter of forms, structures, guidelines, and rules; a hostility to the very thought of change. Of course, *status quo* has been defined by someone as Latin for "the mess we is in." Without doubt, there is great security in maintaining the *status quo*. But God has not called Christians to security, but to sacrifice and service. The Christian faith began on the basis of the most radical change in the history of the world: the abandonment of 1500 years of Mosaic legislation for the revelation of truth and grace which is to be found in the incarnate Christ and the inspired documents of the New Testament.

At the heart of this problem is our inability to think principially rather than mechanically. We fail to see that, while the message is inflexible, the methodology is versatile. Within Biblical parameters methods may change without compromise. This refusal to govern our thinking by principles means that we begin to absolutize non-absolutes so that methods become tyrants rather than servants. The result is that authentic ministry is actually stifled by the idolization of one particular method.

Authentic fundamentalists have always recognized the priority of principles over rules and forms in the development of the Christian life and ministry. A rule or form is a temporal regulation or vehicle which changes with the evolution of culture and the passing of time. A principle, on the other hand, is a foundational truth which is eternal and immutable, and which transcends all cultures and all times. Rules, structures, forms, and guidelines will and must change to increase efficiency in fulfilling God's purposes without compromise. Principles never change.

Those of us within a fundamentalist framework know this to be true. In the 1960's, beards, bell-bottoms, and wire-rim glasses were taboo in many of our churches and educational agencies. And this was not altogether without its reasons. At least some of these seemingly innocent and innocuous items had been announced by the social revolutionaries as the symbols of the revolution. It was probably appropriate in the throes of the 1960's to ban these symbols from Biblical environs. But thirty years later such mores have little relevance and have been abandoned in most of our churches. Rules, structures, forms, and guidelines change; principles do not.

Mechanical thinking develops through a series of five steps. First, there is *truth*—the eternal utterance of God revealed in Scripture. Second, there is *mode*—the channel through which truth expresses itself. Third, there is *practice*—the structured formations of mode. Fourth, there is *tradition*—the entrenchment of practice. And fifth, there is *truth*—the perception by traditionalists that the tradition carries with it divine authority. Perhaps the following chart will be helpful in visualizing this development:

TRUTH >	MODE >	PRACTICE >	TRADITION >	TRUTH >
LOVE FOR THE LOST	EVANGELISTIC OUTREACH	STRUCTURED PROGRAM	"WE'VE ALWAYS DONE IT THIS WAY!"	"PAUL DID IT THIS WAY!"
THE COMMANDMENT OF GOD		THE TRADITION OF MEN		
DEFENDING THIS IS THINKING PRINCIPIALLY		INSISTING ON THIS IS THINKING MECHANICALLY		
FORMS AND STRUCTURES ARE ADAPTED TO CURRENT NEEDS		FORMS AND STRUCTURES ARE ELEVATED TO A DOCTRINAL LEVEL AND PLACED IN CEMENT		
THIS IS *GOD-REVEALED TRUTH: "TRUE TRUTH"*		THIS IS *MAN-DEVELOPED TRUTH: "TEMPORAL TRUTH"*		

This means that some people who are defending man-developed truth actually think that they are defending God-revealed truth. The truth they are defending is really four steps removed from what God said, and, on occasion, may bear very little resemblance to what God said. The real tragedy is that God's commandments are actually frustrated while our own traditions prevail.

So the task of the authentic fundamentalist is to take the eternal principles of Scripture and apply them to the real-life situations of his culture and times, allowing these principles to dictate the forms and structures through which he carries out his ministry and the rules and guidelines by which he lives out his life. This permits adaptations of his ministry to his culture without contamination of his ministry by his culture. This procedure requires careful thought and meticulous study. While there is an abundance of keen minds within Fundamenalism, too many have been content to allow others to do their thinking for them. This has led to a guru mentality among those who are perceived as the thinkers, and a spirit of serfdom among those who become their vassals. No doubt there is a momentary safety in this kind of ecclesiastical feudalism, but there is also a permanent danger, for ultimately it leads to the corruption of the gurus and the rebellion of the vassals. The only protection against this feudalistic system is a return to the priesthood of every believer in which every Spirit-filled, Bible-based priest determines God's principles and then fleshes them out practically in his life and ministry.

Preaching Personal Inventions rather than God's Revelation

Some of us have fallen into the abyss of preaching impositionally rather than expositionally. To preach impositionally means to impose our thoughts on the text rather than to derive God's thoughts from the text. Perhaps the greatest contradiction in

Fundamentalism has been this dialectic of embracing the highest view of inspiration while failing to practice the highest level of communication. In fact, in some sectors of Fundamentalism it might be accurate to say that we have degenerated to the lowest levels of communication. It's too easy to take a text and "take a fit." If Scripture were only a compilation of human thoughts about God composed by religious men, such an approach to preaching would be pardonable. But since Scripture is a revelation of divine truth from God revealed to holy men under the superintendence of the Holy Spirit, such an approach to preaching is unpardonable. The humble task of the preacher is to spend his life telling his people what somebody else said, namely, God! Too many men who are loyal to the task of defending the inspired word are traitors to the task of proclaiming it. God has not called us to invent our messages out of our own minds but to discover them in His Word. This will require a discipline which is prepared to endure the tedium of careful exegesis and diligent study so that we can speak God's Word with authority.

The blessing of God is not for either the demagogue or the orator, who by the skillful use of emotion and prejudice can manipulate vast audiences and hold them spellbound. Instead, the blessing of God is for the Spirit-filled expositor, who spends his life discerning accurately and delivering passionately, relevantly, and clearly the content of God's Word to His people. God's blessing rests supremely with those who take quite literally Paul's mandate: *"Preach the Word"* (II Timothy 4:2). Anything else is infinitely too little.

Equating Mechanical Codes of Conduct with Biblical Holiness

We are not suggesting here that codes of conduct are intrinsically wrong, only that they fall far short of producing true spirituality. On an institutional level, in particular, it is clear that codes of conduct are a definite necessity because multiples of people can only mean multiples of problems. Institutions need a Biblical *purpose* undergirded by Biblical *principles* and implemented by practical *policies*. While all such policies should honor the spirit of the principles and contribute to the fulfillment of the purpose, it is not likely that they will all be linked to a proof text in Scripture. Especially in this kind of circumstance there must be constant reminders that mere outward conformity can never produce sincere inward reality.

One of the grave problems associated with a focus on externals is the development of a preoccupation with the trivial. And the greatest danger of concentrating on the trivial is the ignoring of the vital. That was Jesus' burden in Matthew 23:23: *Woe unto you, scribes and Pharisees, hypocrites! for ye pay tithe of mint and anise and cummin, and have omitted the weightier matters of the law, judgment, mercy, and faith: these ought ye to have done, and not to leave the other undone.*" Jesus indicts the Pharisees for tithing on the herbs of the kitchen garden (the trivial) while simultaneously neglecting justice, mercy, and fidelity (the vital).

To put this in modern terms, a man might dress modestly, groom conservatively, give liberally, pray correctly, attend faithfully and still be a "jerk" spiritually. Why is that? Because he is constantly focusing on the trivial and ignoring the vital. While he is conforming to the external ritual, he is at the very same moment *unjust* in his business—cheating, exploiting and manipulating to improve his bottom line; *unmerciful* in human relationships—cold and indifferent to his spouse and children; and *unfaithful* to his oaths, pledges, and promises with no intention of keeping his word, if it does not suit his purposes.

This kind of hypocrisy will not do for authentic Christians. So while we are holding on to high personal standards which are based on holy Biblical principles, we must never confuse Biblical holiness with mechanical codes of conduct.

Failing to Express Holiness
and Love Simultaneously

If ever there were a balance desperately needed in Christian ministry it is this. We need to develop the skill of expressing compassion without giving way to compromise. This is not easy. That's why we avoid it. It's much easier to opt for one or the other—holiness *or* love rather than holiness *and* love. But this unbiblical imbalance has been destructive to Christ's cause. Most evangelicals have opted for unholy love, and too many fundamentalists have opted for unloving holiness. The imbalance in evangelicalism has produced "sloppy agape," and the imbalance in Fundamentalism has produced "haughty holiness." Both of these extremes are distortions of the image of God in which we are made and of which we are to be reflectors. God is not "sloppy" when He expresses *agape* and neither is He "haughty" when He expresses His holiness. Failure to express holiness and love simultaneously turns God's people and God's servants into eccentric caricatures instead of authentic pictures of the Christ we represent.

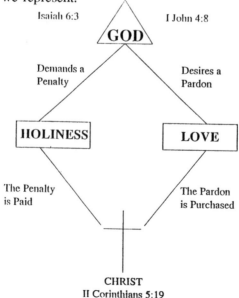

Isaiah 6:3   GOD   I John 4:8

Demands a
Penalty   Desires a
                                          Pardon

HOLINESS   LOVE

The Penalty
is Paid   The Pardon
                                          is Purchased

CHRIST
II Corinthians 5:19

While some tend to think of holiness and love as competing attributes of God, I see them as complementary. Paul weds them inseparably in I Thessalonians 3:12 and 13 when he states that abounding love results in unblamable holiness. Clearly they are not incompatible, but inseparable.

To express holiness and love simultaneously requires sacrifice. How do we know this? The supreme demonstration of holiness and love expressed simultaneously is the cross of Christ, the place of ultimate *sacrifice*. It was there that both holiness and love were satisfied. The penalty holiness demanded was paid, and the pardon love desired was purchased.

So we, too, will have to be sacrificial. Some of us tend to harshness and pharisaism—it will have to be crucified! Some of us tend to softness and sentamentalism—it will have to be crucified! It's costly to maintain this delicate balance. Perhaps that's why there are so few Christians who bother. But without this sacrificial investment, we can never be the authentic Christians we are called to be, nor shall we be able to develop the authentic ministries we are called to develop!

Affirming Our Views before Exegeting God's Word

It is sometimes true that we talk before we think. On occasion there have been those among us who have blurted out demands without feeling the necessity to justify them. Only God has such a right. All the rest of us are obliged to explain why. And if we don't, before long human affirmations begin to eclipse divine affirmations so that men end up speaking with the same authority as God. Too often the touchstone for truth and ministry is neither Christ nor His Word, but the regional guru. This simply won't do if we intend to engage in authentic, Biblical ministry. To be sure, it is not intrinsically wrong to be affirmational. No true fundamentalist is timid about affirming his beliefs. But he is always certain that before he opens his mouth to the world in public, he has first opened his mind to the Word in private.

Unfortunately, fundamentalists have not always been the standard bearers for this kind of exegesis. On too many occasions, statements about theological positions and ecclesiastical personalities have been made which later proved to be indefensible. This has led not only to embarrassment for the cause, but also, in some cases, to wholesale defection from it. It seems to me that our loyalty to Scripture demands that we defer to its authority over our lives. This will require a changing of our minds if we judge that our previous affirmations have not been exegetically sound or precisely accurate. This is the kind of humility which God promises to bless. And once we have gone through this process, we can combine confidence in the views we hold with humility and compassion in the way we express them.

Condemning Sins of the Flesh while Overlooking Sins of the Spirit

Sins of the flesh are overt, like David's sin with Bathsheba. They most often find their source in lust and greed. Sins of the spirit are covert, like David's sin of numbering the people. They most often find their source in pride and arrogance. Which of these two sins of David did God judge most severely? A careful study of the record shows that four people died as a direct result of David's sin of the flesh (the infant, Amnon, Absalom, and Adonijah), whereas 70,000 people died as a direct result of David's sin of the spirit (I Chronicles 21:13-14). As someone has suggested, there are both prodigal sons (sins of the flesh) and elder brothers (sins of the spirit). The prodigal son wasted his life groveling in the world; the elder brother wasted his life grumbling at home.

Our failure has been in refusing to see that sins of the spirit are just as destructive to God's work as sins of the flesh (II Corinthians 7:1). In fact, sometimes they are even more destructive! While we have taken strong stands against gross immorality, we have on occasion actually engaged in the finer sins of Jesuit ethics, power politics, prideful boasting, malicious gossip, and diabolical slander. Sometimes we have actually employed these tactics in the defense of the faith. But such carnal weaponry will no longer do for authentic fundamentalists. In the words of Paul: *". . . the weapons of our warfare are not carnal, but mighty through God to the pulling down of strongholds"* (II Corinthians 10:4). This juxtaposition of "carnal" and "mighty" weaponry may suggest that we rob our weapons of divine power whenever we employ fleshly tactics to achieve righteous goals. It is an unfortunate reality of history that questionable strategies have been employed by some of our fundamentalist forebears in the midst of battles with apostasy and compromise. The justification for such strategies was the righteous objectives of those employing them. But how does this differ from the Jesuit ethics (noble ends justify cunning and hypocritical means)?

Fighting fire with fire is a useful dictum for those who fight forest fires, but not for God's truth proclaimers and standard bearers! It will do neither us nor the cause of Christ any good to feign the defense of the Bible while we are at the same moment denying the integrity of the Bible by violating its ethical principles.

How can we avoid fleshly tactics and ethical compromise in our struggle to defend truth in a hostile world? It will require of us accuracy in factual data before indicting those with whom we disagree. Ethical propriety would also demand the kind of integrity which secures the right to quote private correspondence before printing it in some tabloid. It demands of us the kind of diligence which probes original sources for information and statistics regarding movements and people who contradict fundamentalist theology, rather than relying on second-hand information. And finally, ethical integrity would certainly lay upon us the responsibility to provide constructive fundamentalist alternatives, which are both innovative and Biblical, to the compromising ministries which we oppose.

The time has come for all true fundamentalists to acknowledge that doctrinal correctness is never a justification for ethical corruption. Authentic fundamentalists must renew their loyalty to the utilization of God's divine weaponry, their antipathy for the employment of carnal weaponry and their fidelity to the exercise of transparent Biblical ethics and attitudes in all that they do.

Neglecting to Apply Christian Truth to Cultural Issues

Fundamentalists have tended to limit the application of Christian truth to personal life styles while failing to see its application to the great cultural issues of our day. There are occasions when we will have to turn our attention away from such things as hem lines and hair lengths (and there is a place for dealing with modesty in both dress and grooming—Paul and Peter did!) and to focus on such issues as encroaching secularism, avaricious materialism, pervasive evolutionism and defiant feminism. God's Word speaks profoundly to all of these issues, and there is no doubt that each one of them has made a radical impact on the values of our culture and in many cases on the values of Christian people. If God's Word speaks to these issues, so should we. Many Christians come to church with confused ideas and they are wondering "Is there any word from God?" on such matters. We must let them know that there is.

It is probably safe to say that the Christian mind is firmly anchored to four unchangeable truths, four great realities, which are found in God's Word and which enable Christians to think clearly in the midst of incredible complexity. This is an advantage which no other religionist or philosopher possesses and Christians would be foolish not to capitalize upon it. These great realities can be defined as (1) the Creation (the good); (2) the Fall (the evil); (3) the Redemption (the new); and (4) the Consummation (the perfect). As one author put it:

This four-fold Biblical reality enables Christians to survey the historical landscape within its proper horizons. It supplies the true perspective from which to view the unfolding process between two eternities, the vision of God working out His purpose. It gives us a framework in which to fit everything, a way of integrating our understanding, the possibility of thinking straight, even about the most complex issues.[3]

So then, only Christians, who look at life through the lens of these four realities, can understand realistically what is happening in their culture and prescribe meaningfully the solutions to the complexities we face. If it is true that *"Righteousness exalteth a nation: but sin is a reproach to any people"* (Proverbs 14:34), then God's righteous people must confront the sin which is all around them with His unchangeable and powerful truth.

For my part, I believe this should be done less through socio-political activism and more through a dynamic network of independent, fundamental, local churches. I believe we have vastly underestimated the power of a Spirit-controlled, God-honoring expositor of Scripture who is ministering to a revived people. We need prophetic voices ministering to authentic Christians, voices which are unafraid to thunder out the eternal principles of God's divine Word. The effect will be that not only our individual lives, but also our cultural ills, will be touched and transformed. When this kind of pungent salt is rubbed into the cultural decadence and this kind of brilliant light shines into the cultural darkness, we can be sure that lasting individual and cultural impacts will be made.

Measuring by Counting
rather than by Weighing

For more than a quarter of a century, we have labored under the false assumption that bigness equals greatness and that success can be measured quantitatively. We are much more effective at counting numbers than weighing ideas. This is a form of secularization and an indication that we have bought into the affluence mentality of our day. We seem always to be thinking in terms of numbers, numbers, numbers! How much? How many? How big? This push has led to the disintegration of ethics in reporting statistics and represents a tragic failure to recognize that invisible spiritual growth cannot be accurately gauged by mechanical measuring devices. Moreover, it forms the ground of pragmatism which has invaded so much of Christian ministry. The trouble with pragmatism is that it works: it attracts large crowds. But under its influence, we end up "succeeding miserably" because we are not succeeding Biblically.

In many cases the result has been the development of a philosophy of ministry which revolves around a celebrity focus (the star of the show who attracts the crowd) who functions as a corporate executive manipulating and then discarding his people in his relentless advance toward statistical superiority. All too often, evangelism in this context has been reduced to humanism as the Spirit and the Word are set aside while the Gospel is packaged and marketed almost as though it were a plastic toy.

The passing of time, however, has demonstrated that artificial methodology can never produce authentic ministry. Super-dooper facilities and super-star personalities have begun to unravel in the last 5–10 years. Churches, and in some cases whole movements, have begun to cave-in and collapse. The kinds of abuses which accompany this philosophy of ministry have produced a wasteland, a desert of the spirit among God's people. Many souls who were once aflame with joyful enthusiasm have now been reduced to dead ashes. Both pastors and people have become sick, empty and burned out.

Quite frankly, I believe that we have gotten the cart before the horse. Emaciated women cannot give birth to healthy children. Neither can emaciated Christians. Perhaps we should take more seriously Paul's emphasis that the marks of a mature church are *"faith, hope, and love"* (I Corinthians 13:13; Ephesians 1:15,16,18; Colossians 1:3-6; II Thessalonians 1:3,4). Whatever else we judge to be a sign of maturity or an evidence of success, all else is meaningless apart from these more fundamental and Scriptural indicators. Perhaps it would be more honest when computing our statistics of how many our pragmatic methods brought in, to compute alongside them how many they drove away. Perhaps it would be more Biblically accurate when calculating our numerics, to list how many husbands are lovingly leading their wives, how many wives are humbly following their husbands, and how many children are cheerfully obeying their parents. Faith, hope, love—authentic husbands, wives, and children, these are the measuring devices by which we should be gauging the success of our ministries. And when such qualities become a reality in our churches, all the rest will follow quite naturally: growth will come!

It may take a good long while before many of us will be able to root out of our own thinking these false systems of computing success, but it is an effort we must all make if we ever hope to return to authentic New Testament Christianity.

So these are the hindrances to a balanced Fundamentalism. They are many and varied but they are not irremediable. The next generation of fundamentalists must aspire, under God and in His power, to see these super- structural deformities repaired while refusing to abandon their doctrinal foundations. If they do, a powerful new force for God and good will emerge in twentieth- and twenty-first century America.

CHAPTER TWO

IDENTIFYING TRUE LEADERSHIP

"At the appearance of Christ it will be made manifest who Christians really are for they shall share in His glory. But there are some who simply cannot, or will not, wait. They lust to be known, to be named now, and so instead of waiting for Christ's kingdom, they have decided to build their own!"

This is the age of power ethics and like a tragic infection or epidemic disease we are all susceptible to its influence. Everywhere we look we see evidences of this disease. On the *personal* level, it is evident in the human quest for independence or autonomy, our desire to cast off all forms of restraint and be free to do our "own thing," or as David put it: *"Let us break their bands asunder, and cast away their cords from us"* (Psalm 2:3). On the *corporate* level you can see it in the form of ruthless business tactics motivated by a bottom-line mentality. On the *political* level it becomes apparent in the growth of bloated governments like our own, which seem always to be hungering for more and more money and control, and in the rise of gangster leaders like Hitler and Stalin a generation ago and like Sadaam Hussein or the Eastern European leaders who have recently been exposed and expelled in the contemporary world.

Politics, in particular, provides a fertile context for the abuse of power. Charles Colson, Richard Nixon's supposed hatchet man, supplies a graphic illustration of this. On Nixon's last presidential trip abroad in June, 1974, he was accompanied by two senior aides, Al Haig and Ron Ziegler, both of whom were vying for the top position in the Nixon administration. The trip, which began in the Soviet Union and included stops in Iran and Israel, was a vain last-ditch effort to divert attention away from the president's political crisis. By that time everyone knew Mr. Nixon couldn't survive the public clamor more than another month or two; his entire administration was about to collapse. Nevertheless, the advance team was equipped with tape measures and meticulous instructions to insure that in all sleeping accommodations Mr. Ziegler's and Mr. Haig's beds would be equidistant from the president's.[1] These men lusted for access to the corridors of power and hungered for the appearance of power even though it was in the process of decay and disintegration. Here were world leaders acting like little boys who are infected with a form of egomania.

But we must face ourselves squarely here. The problem of power is not limited to pagans and politicians; it impacts preachers and professors too. It's in the hearts of all of Adam's race, and, if we were perfectly honest, we should have to admit that it lurks in our hearts too. In fact, its abuse can be found almost everywhere in all human relationships. In the home, in the form of a domineering and abusive parent or a rebellious and self-centered child. On the job, in the form of an abrasive superior or an insubordinate subordinate. In marriage, in the form of an exploitive chauvinism or an assertive feminism. And even in the church, in the form of a spiritual leader who likes to play God or a Diotrophes who intends to beat him at his own game.

It is too often true that the demeanor of those who occupy positions of spiritual leadership smacks of royalty and that their view of the church borders on ownership. They seem, almost, to be breathing rarified air, so high is their view of themselves. But it is Christ's church not ours, for He purchased it with His own blood, and it is only He who wears the *diadema* (the royal crown). The rest of us are privileged to earn the *stephanoi* (the wreath of the olympian), but the royal crown belongs only to Him. The quickest way to forfeit authentic and joyful ministry is to try to own what belongs to God alone (Acts 20:28; I Peter 5:3; Ecclesiastes 2:18-21).

While we chuckle at Pharisaical abuses of power, aren't we so often just like them? We, too, are very sensitive about our placement at meetings around tables and on platforms and are often quite insistent that our placement match with our rank in the hierarchy. Isn't it true that we want to catch the public eye and have them see us in the position of prominence or at least in the shadow of greatness? Jesus condemned the Pharisees for longing to be seen of men and loving *"the uppermost rooms at feasts, and the chief seats in the synagogues, and greetings in the markets, and to be called of men, Rabbi, Rabbi* [my great one, my great one]" (Matthew 23:5-7). This longing for prominence and loving of preeminence is in every one of us. We shall have to be very careful lest we fall under the same scathing denunciation from Christ that the Pharisees received.

There are those moments when we hunger to be the answer man, the one to whom everyone comes for counsel. And when we give the answer we expect to bask in their adulation and admiration. How foolish! All the real answers are God's, not ours. Accepting such adulation and admiration would be like the donkey carrying Jesus into Jerusalem on Palm Sunday believing that the crowds were cheering and laying down their garments and palm branches for him.[2] I fear that there are too many occasions when we play the part of the donkey and forget that we are called to be humble bearers of Christ's message and transparent reflectors of His image, exalting Him not ourselves.

So what is the answer to this infection of power-ethics? Simply stated, it is the rejection of the Luciferian formula cited by Milton in *Paradise Lost*: "Better to *reign* in Hell than to *serve* in Heaven." Nothing is more demeaning to Satan than service and nothing is more appealing than sovereignty. But if we are to reject the Luciferian formula in order to overcome the terrible infection of power, we shall also have to embrace the Biblical formula for Christian servitude which was personified in Christ and penned by the apostle Paul (Philippians 2:5-8).

The Tragedy of Power Seeking

Many fundamentalists seem to have an Adam-like hunger for God-like power. The corruptive influence of power, which we once thought touched only the unregenerate masses, materialistic corporations, and gluttonous politicians, has found its way into the underlying framework of Christian organizations as well. This has resulted in a reliance upon "proper pedigree, positions of status, and connections among those in the power structure," rather than confidence in the sovereignty of the Spirit and the will of God.[3] These very items, which constitute a false reliance, are precisely what Paul called "dung" (Philippians 3:8) and in which he had absolutely no confidence (Philippians 3:3). Is it possible that we, in our day, are reverting to such thinking by placing our confidence in fleshly means of ascending to positions of power? Clearly, authentic servant-leaders will find it necessary to reject such means, while they learn to rely completely upon the Holy Spirit for His direction in their lives.

How does "power" work? What are the dynamics of power? How does it get its grip on us and how can we protect ourselves from its corruptive influence? We shall attempt to answer at least some of these questions in the following pages.

Dynamics of Power

First, we shall try to deal with the *dynamics of power*. By the use of the word "dynamics" I have in mind the moving forces or moral motions within this illusive entity, which make it so attractive to us and at the same moment so destructive. It is not an easy subject to define, but its importance justifies the attempt. For our purposes here we will be looking at only two of the basic dynamics of power against which all authentic servants of God must rigorously guard themselves.

Ladder Climbing

The first dynamic of power which seems to have a gripping, compelling attraction for far too many of us involved in Christian service is what I have chosen to call *ladder climbing*. It is an unfortunate reality that power structures tend to grow up around significant ministries and personalities. Infrastructures (internal administrative networks) begin to develop with their committees, platforms, pulpits and boards, and these become *the ecclesiastical corporate ladder*, which will lead you to "the top" so long as you play the game according to the rules. And what does it mean to play the game according to the rules? It means showing up at all the right meetings, speaking to all the right people and saying all the right things. In this way we make ourselves visible and move up the ladder.

More precisely, how is this behavior to be defined? I think we all know it by another title: politics! If we are not careful, these structures and the ladders which they provide can turn authentic servant leaders into political power seekers in a very short period of time.

And with politics comes the inevitable infection of strife, which has become in some circles, at least, the hallmark of Fundamentalism. As a matter of fact, the Bible word for "strife" *(eritheia)* is a political word. It describes the contention which is born of envy; the desire for prestige and a place of prominence. It portrays a careerist or opportunist who lusts for officialdom and is not above the use of Gospel preaching for personal empire building. One book defines this word as denoting "a self-seeking pursuit of political office by unfair means . . . . party squabbles . . . . jockeying for position and the intriguing for place and power . . . . selfish ambition, the ambition which has no conception of service and whose only aims are profit and power."[4] Such are the ugly deformities of power politics in a Christian context. It is difficult to imagine anything more incompatible with the spirit and ethic of Jesus Christ.

If you can visualize the phenomenon of Fundamentalism as a large circle, it may not be too difficult to visualize a number of smaller circles within it which symbolize the lesser kingdoms which have grown up within the larger circle over the years. In the strictest sense, these smaller circles are not intrinsically wrong. They represent regional ministries located in various parts of the country. It's only when they become self-contained, self-serving and self-centered kingdoms that they become divisive and hurtful. We know this is happening when "my cause" becomes more important than "the cause." In that kind of milieu our respective ministries seem always to be cast in the mold of being competitors rather than compatriots. Compatriots recognize their identity as members of the same great kingdom; competitors have eyes and a heart for only their own little kingdom! Instead of networking with those of "like precious faith" in order to serve Christ's cause, we tend to engage in stone throwing in order to protect our turf and serve our cause.

However, this form of ladder climbing, our self-centered attempts to move up the ecclesiastical corporate ladder of the regional kingdom, is replete with all kinds of problems.

Is Jesus Christ still Lord?

First and foremost among these problems is that the lordship of Jesus Christ of Nazareth gets lost in the dust! A man might be prompted by the Spirit and the Word to develop in his community a ministry which is definitely unconventional but clearly not unbiblical; something that is not deviate, just different. So who does he think of first? It was God who prompted him, but who is going to control him? Will it be Jesus Christ or the local guru? All too often it is our Lord Jesus Christ who is dismissed so that we can keep climbing the ladder. Authentic ministry is forfeited so that the pursuit of power can be perpetuated.

Are we identifying with the early Christians or the Pharisees?

The second problem associated with ladder climbing is that it is very much unlike primitive Christianity. It is interesting to see in the book of Acts "the clash between powerless officials and official-less power."[5] The Pharisees enjoyed the privileges of officialdom, but it was the apostles and their followers who experienced the power of God. We shall all have to decide which *we* want: the privileges of officialdom, or the blessings of divine power channeled through our lives and ministries. I am convinced that in twentieth century Fundamentalism we could all prosper from a return to official-less power. This kind of power is more a matter of disposition than position; of attitude than rank.

It would be both unwise and unbiblical to suggest that the exercise of power is somehow intrinsically wrong for it clearly isn't, or that structures of authority have no place in Christian ministry for they clearly do. Official-less power then, can only mean that when God's servants exercise the power with which they have been entrusted by God Himself, they must do so in the interests of "the cause" not "my cause"; they must visualize others in similar fundamentalist ministries as compatriots not competitors; and they must insist upon servant leadership as the model of true spirituality in Christian ministry. In this way, God-given power can be exercised without being exploited. Christ gave to those New Testament Christians "power without a kingdom, power without a position."[6] Just before the ascension they were bold to ask: *"wilt thou at this time restore again the kingdom to Israel?"* (Acts 1:6). And Christ's answer was, *"No. that is for later."* But in the interim *"ye shall receive power, after that the Holy Ghost is come upon you"* (Acts 1:8). And this is a power which would enable them to meet the needs of others locally (Jerusalem), regionally (Judea), cross-culturally (Samaria) and internationally (the uttermost part of the earth). There is a desperate need for this kind of need-meeting power, as opposed to ladder-climbing power, within the hearts and ministries of all of us who aspire to be authentic servants of God.

Is this a duplication of the world?

But there is a third problem associated with ladder climbing. Not only is it inconsistent with the lordship of Christ and the life style of New Testament Christianity, it is also an imitation of the world system. The symbols of God's power are not "bravado and bombast." These are the symbols of human power, the power of this fallen cosmos. It's not scratch, clutch, grasp, manipulate, exploit, dig in, step on, and climb over! That's the world's way, yet on far too many occasions these are the machinations which have characterized the "power politics" of modern Christendom, including even certain segments of Fundamentalism. On the contrary, the symbols of God's power are "a manger and a cross."[7] What could be more vulnerable or more powerless than a newborn baby in a manger or a crucified man on a cross, yet the incarnation (the manger) and the crucifixion (the cross) were both works of great *power*. The most powerful thing Jesus of Nazareth ever did was to assume our humanness in the incarnation and our fallenness in the crucifixion. Likewise, real power is released into and then out of us when we are prepared to identify with sinners (as Christ did in the incarnation) and sacrificially give ourselves to meet their needs (as Christ did in the crucifixion). Yet how many contemporary Christians are interested in either sinners or a cross?

Resisting Christ's lordship, betraying the New Testament model, and conforming to the world system—these are the grave problems which attach themselves to ladder climbing. And these are the reasons no authentic servant of God should ever succumb to the allurements of power.

Name Seeking

But if the first dynamic of power is ladder climbing, the second is *name seeking*. We aspire to be named in order to achieve a sense of identity and self-worth. And it is this hunger which makes us most vulnerable to power.[8] We want to be named, to be known *as* something or *for* something and we are convinced that our identity, our self-worth is bound up in the name. And if we can't get a name of our own, then we want to be name droppers. That is a form of vicarious power; deriving power by some form of association with the powerful.[9] If somehow we can demonstrate that we have a link to the inner circle, we can bask in the ambiance of power, if not in the actual experience of it.

But what is the true source of meaningful identity and significant worth? Is it in the name we *achieve* through our selfish struggle for personal recognition, or the name we *receive* through our selfless submission to spiritual conversion? To me the answer is obvious. When we become Christians we are named! We are sons of God *(huios)*, servants of God *(diakonos)* and slaves of God *(doulos)*. Beyond this, we are priests, judges, and saints. Isn't this enough? Not for many, because as yet such realities are not *visible* to the watching world, and that is the one thing so many of God's servants want—they want to be visible, to be seen, to be known, to be named! Why? Because they believe there is power in such visibility and such notoriety— in such a name!

Paul has an interesting insight in this connection in Colossians 3:3-4. He states that now our *"life is hid with Christ in God"* (verse 3). Among other things, that means that our true identity as the people of God is not immediately evident to the world. They are not impressed by our claims to be God's children, nor are they moved to give us a position of status because of them. However, *"when Christ . . . shall appear, then shall ye also appear with Him in glory"* (verse 4). At the appearance of Christ, it will be made manifest who Christians really are, for they shall share in His glory. But there are some who simply cannot, or will not, wait. They lust to be known, to be named now. Therefore, instead of waiting for Christ's kingdom, they have decided to build their own!

It is possible for us to argue that a name and the power which it provides will enable us to do great good for the cause of Christ. But that argument is only a deception. In a sense, this was Satan's strategy in the temptation of Christ in the wilderness. The devil showed Christ all the kingdoms of the world and then said to Him, *"All this power will I give thee, and the glory of them: for that is delivered unto me; and to whomsoever I will give it. If thou therefore wilt worship me, all shall be thine"* (Luke 4:6-7). Some have seen this as Satan saying to Christ: "Look at the good you could do with power," while Jesus seems to be replying, "with all that power, good would go sour."[10] And isn't that precisely what has happened so much in recent years? With all that power, good has soured in more than one Christian ministry, both within and without Fundamentalism.

Besides, Scripture makes it very clear that it is with God's name and not our own that we should be preoccupied. All through the Old Testament we read of "the Name," and in the New Testament from the lips of our Lord Jesus Christ Himself we are taught to pray, *"Hallowed be thy name . . . thy kingdom . . . thy will,"* not my name, my kingdom, my will. Perhaps that's why the Chronicler records this:

> *"Thine, O Lord, is the greatness, and the power, and the glory, and the victory, and the majesty: for all that is in the heaven and in the earth is thine; thine is the kingdom, O Lord, and thou art exalted as head above all. Both riches and honor come of thee, and thou reignest over all; and in thine hand is power and might; and in thine hand it is to make great, and to give strength unto all. Now therefore, our God, we thank thee, and praise thy glorious name"* (I Chronicles 29:11-13).

In that passage there are six references to *thine* and none to *mine*. With a name like His, God will have none of the exaltation of a name like ours! On a practical basis, what this means is that we must learn to say from our hearts with John the Baptist, *"He must increase, but I must decrease";* and equally as important we must say with John: *"I am not the Christ"* (John 3:28,30). These are such relevant statements because the grave danger of both ladder climbers and name seekers is that they tend to become messianic in their outlook. In such a context it is most appropriate that we should exalt Christ and not ourselves, and that we periodically remind our people and ourselves of this sobering truth: "I am not the Christ!"

There can be no doubt that both ladder climbing and name seeking constitute a significant part of the moral motions of power. Our failure to recognize them and protect ourselves against them will have disastrous effects in our personal lives and corporate ministries. If it is true that the fall of man can be cast in the mold of an appeal for power *("ye shall be as gods"* Genesis 3:5); and if it is true that all of Adam's race is infected with Adam's fallenness *("Adam . . . begat a son in his own likeness, after his image"* Genesis 5:3); then it is equally true that we are all liable to the deceptive and destructive influences of power and will have to take specific steps to protect ourselves against its corruptive influence.

Steps for Protection against Deceptive and Destructive Influences of Power

Personally Develop the Mind of Christ

First, we shall have to develop a *kenosis mentality* (Philippians 2:5-8). Since this is a concept which will be developed in some detail later in this chapter, we shall only mention it briefly here. The "mind of Christ," which we are obligated to embrace, is a *kenosis mind*. It means emptying ourselves to fill others, spending ourselves to serve others and sacrificing ourselves to help others. It means rejecting our preoccupation with our own "reputation" in order to serve Christ, His cause, His church, His creation. In these verses that is precisely what Christ Himself did for us. He emptied Himself and became a man (2:6,7); He spent Himself and became a servant (2:7); He humbled Himself and became a sacrifice (2:8). In all such self-emptying there can be no self-exalting. This is truly a protection against power seeking.

Be a Servant Model

Second, we shall have to *embrace servant models of leadership* (Matthew 20:25-28). Jesus makes it very clear that Christian leadership is fundamentally different from non-Christian leadership: *"ye know that the princes of the Gentiles exercise dominion* [katakurieuo] *over them, and they that are great exercise authority* [katexousiazo] *upon them. But it shall not be so among you . . ."* (20:25,26a). Both of the Greek terms which describe the pagan form of leadership are brutalizing in nature. Literally, they mean "to lord down" and "to authority down." Though the English is awkward, the imagery is accurate. There is tyranny, despotism, and self-serving manipulation in each. While the second term is used only here and in the parallel passage in Mark 10:42, the first term is used in Acts 19:16 of exploitation by demonic beings and in I Peter 5:3 of exploitation by self-serving elders. No wonder the negative particle (not) is emphatic by its placement at the head of the sentence in verse 26. "Not so among you" would be a good way of stating it.

Conversely, in God's kingdom the great are servants *(diakonos)* and the first are slaves *(doulos)*. Anything less than this model for leadership is pagan (the way the Gentiles do things) and a betrayal of Christ's personal example (v. 28). In His life the two key words were *service*, for He came *"not to be ministered unto, but to minister,"* and *sacrifice*, for He came *"to give His life a ransom for many."* This is truly a protection against power seeking.

Be a Team Player

Third, we must seek to *develop a team spirit* in matters of leadership (Acts 13:1). I love the team in Antioch. Think of who they were. There was Barnabas, a real estate magnate who owned property on Cyprus, "the Blessed Isle" and who possessed Levitical roots. There was Simeon, who was clearly a black man, and who may have borne Christ's cross for Him out to Calvary (Mark 15:21). There was Lucius from Cyrene in North Africa, who was probably a black man, too. There was Manaen, who had been one of the intimates of the Herod family and was very much an insider of first century aristocratic society in Palestine. And, finally, there was Saul, a fiery intellectual from Tarsus, with a pharisaical background.[11] How could such men serve together? It is clear that true Christian love was a deep-seated reality in that church and that among the members of the team there was none of that smallness of soul which cannot tolerate a rival. A *prima donna* (Italian for "first lady"—the leading female singer in an opera or concert) is a person who finds it difficult to work under direction or as a part of a team; one who is impatient of restraint or criticism and who demands absolute, uncontested, unquestioning loyalty. None of the Antioch staff were *prima donnas!* It's no wonder that God used this church and staff to launch the first international missionary initiative, which would eventually carry the Gospel to the *"uttermost part of the earth."* A team spirit, which allows for God-ordained structures of authority, but disallows the unbearable and intolerable moods of a *prima donna*, is truly a protection against power seeking.

Be Accountable to Someone

Fourth, we must be willing to *subject ourselves to structures of accountability* (Acts 14:27, 28). It was the church at Antioch which had released Paul to the missionary enterprise (13:3), and it was to that same church that Paul felt obligated to report when he returned. It is never wise in a fallen world to develop concentrations of power which are not subject to some form of earthly balance. Pastors don't operate from an Old Testament theocratic or patriarchal model, where kings and patriarchs possessed absolute, autocratic authority based on direct revelation from heaven. God's kingdom has not yet been erected on earth, and in the interim between Christ's first and second comings, pastors function as shepherds (not kings) of New Testament local churches (not a theocratic kingdom). So while their office is *authoritative* or official as having been established by God Himself, they themselves are not to be *authoritarian*. Webster's definition of "authoritarian" is "favoring a principle of blind submission to authority . . . a set of commands issuing from above, a group of subordinates below to be ordered ruthlessly about." This is demeaning to both the priesthood of every believer and the dignity of the office of the pastor.

In order to protect ourselves from such abuses, it might be wise for Christian leaders to grant to certain trusted and charactered peers the right to tell them when they have stopped being servant leaders and started being power seekers.

Be Content with God's Score Card

Fifth, we should *purpose never to aspire to mega-ministries* (Jeremiah 45:5). It would be wrong to say that mega-ministries are somehow intrinsically evil. They certainly are not. If God ordains them, we have no right to either oppose them or resist them. However, it would be wise to remember that all kinds of subtle temptations lurk all around those who preside over such ministries. A good many men began their ministries as humble servants repudiating vainglory, but ended their ministries as high-minded kings demanding honor from their followers. One of the reasons is their failure to discern and then protect themselves from the corruptive influence of power. I would like to make two suggestions in this regard. Together they might protect us against power's subtle temptations.

How big shall we grow before we divide?

My first suggestion is simply this: there may be some merit in considering a numerical level beyond which a local church will not go without dividing and planting a new church. This would not work well in rural areas, but it might be feasible in urban areas. There are several tangible and immediate blessings which can result from such an approach to ministry: (1) it rejuvenates evangelism due to a loss of people to formulate the nucleus of a new church; (2) it eliminates the necessity of massive facilities and their costly maintenance; (3) it may protect the spiritual leadership from the guru mentality which can develop as one presides over his personal empire. Pastors never find it easy to give away good people. But giving birth to New Testament churches may be just the motivation they need!

Have you counted the cost of notoriety?

My second suggestion is that we should beware of the dangers of being at the top. From a distance, being at the top looks so inviting, but the reality never seems to match the fantasy. Personally, I think there is an advantage to obscurity over notoriety. The reason is this: in obscurity you are *free* to be the slave of Jesus; in notoriety you tend to become the *prisoner* of everybody else's expectations. In obscurity you can be the person God has called you to be and equipped you to be. In notoriety you're expected to be what others perceive you to be and pressure you to be. This does not mean that notoriety may not come to you or your ministry. But if it does come, be certain that it was *God* who promoted, not *you* who pushed yourself ahead (Ps. 75:6,7)! It should be the result of divine providence not human politics. Purposing never to aspire to megaministries, refusing to make that your life goal, can be a significant protection against the corruptive influence of power.

Be Cautious of Hero Worship

Sixth, we must be careful to *avoid excessive adulation of our heroes.* Sometimes we contribute to the corruption of good men by our fawning behavior. The tragedy is that sometimes these heroes actually begin to believe their press releases. Is it wrong for us to have heroes within Fundamentalism? Not intrinsically, although I believe that *models* is a much better term than *heroes.* It is certainly true that we need models of the Christian faith who are worthy of emulation, and the New Testament authors were not afraid to affirm this (I Thessalonians 1:6,7; I Peter 5:3). The problem with so many contemporary heroes is that they are not good models. And, conversely, there are many excellent models who have never been heard of, and, as a result, they are nobody's heroes.

But whether we opt for models or heroes, we must guard ourselves against excessive adulation. J. Oswald Sanders was right to say "Acceptance of fawning deference by a leader is a weakness. He must studiously refuse to be idolized." This is certainly true, but those of us who do the fawning are partially to blame for the corruption it breeds in otherwise good men. Here, too, we must be cautious!

Be Aware of Satan's Tactics

Finally, we must *learn ways of defeating the powers of evil.* It is not without significance that almost all the terms which are used to describe demonic beings in Scripture have something to do with power! Paul provides a precise and picturesque portrait of our spiritual enemies in Ephesians 6:11-12. In this passage he lists four frightening qualities of demonic beings: (1) they are *spiritual*—*"For we wrestle not against flesh and blood;"* (2) they are *resourceful*—for he can speak of *"the wiles* [*methodeias*—deceitful and scheming craftiness] *of the devil;"* (3) they are *powerful*—for he names them, *"principalities . . . powers . . . rulers;"* (4) and they are *immoral*—for they lurk in *"darkness"* and engage in *"wickedness."*

What is of particular relevance to our discussion is the fact that demonic beings are powerful. Paul's descriptive terms leave no doubt at all that we are facing an impressive array of power. Principalities *(archas)* means the moving power, the dynamic force which sets something into operation. Powers *(exousias)* describes the power to add and the power to take away at will; it is a sophisticated power, the kind exercised in the world of legal, political, social, or moral affairs. Rulers *(kosmokratoras)* means literally, world rulers. It suggests controlling completely and vanquishing utterly whatever it has in its clutches. "The principalities and powers do not just have power—they *are* power. They exist as power; power is how they manifest themselves. To dominate, to control, to devour, to imprison, is their very essence."[12] So we face not only the monster within, our Adam-like hunger for God-like power, but also the demons without, a frightening and powerful array of enemies. What must we do to defeat them? Foster suggests several steps that I find challenging (189-193).

Recognize Christ's Victory

First, we must recognize that Christ has already defeated them (Colossians 2:15), and that the ground of our victory over evil and the evil one is to be found in our union with Him.

Cultivate Discernment

Second, we defeat the powers of evil by cultivating the gift of discernment (I Corinthians 12:10; I John 4:1). While some may be uniquely endowed to carry out this task, all Christians are responsible to be discerning: judging claims, experiences, and our own personal appetites by the touchstone of Scripture.

Face Personal Character Flaws

Third, we must uncompromisingly face the monsters within: not demons per se, who cannot possess Christians (I John 4:4), but demonic appetites and attitudes such as greed, violence, fear, hate, and the lust for power itself. These are the powers which nip at our own heels, and which we must face honestly and uncompromisingly.

Reject Control by Things

Fourth, we defeat the powers by an internal repudiation of all things except our union with God. In such a condition we have nothing to lose; the powers have no control over us. Before people who in their hearts are positionless and possessionless the powers are powerless!

Renounce Carnal Weaponry

The powers become defeatable when we renounce carnal weaponry. That's Paul's burden when he says: *"For though we walk in the flesh, we do not war after the flesh: (For the weapons of our warfare are not carnal, but mighty through God to the pulling down of strong holds)"* (II Corinthians 10:3-4). The powers seek to manipulate, dominate, and intimidate in order to control. Such weapons will not do for us. We shall have to confront *"principalities . . . powers . . . world-rulers"* in the power of the Holy Spirit. Only then can we expect victory.

Master Divine Weaponry

Finally, in defeating the powers we must master the use of the divine weaponry prescribed in Ephesians 6:14-17. We shall have to lay hold of the belt of truth because Satan is a liar; the breastplate of righteousness because Satan is an accuser; the boots of the gospel of peace because Satan is a warrior; the shield of faith because Satan is an archer; the helmet of salvation because Satan is a beguiler; and the sword of the Spirit because Satan is a murderer. Armed with truth, righteousness, peace, faith, salvation, and the Word of God the humblest of Christians becomes an undefeatable foe of the evil one and his emissaries. And it is as we learn and implement all of these ways of defeating the powers of evil that we simultaneously protect ourselves and others from the corruptive influences of power itself!

The Triumph of Servant Leading

In 1986 the incoming freshman class at Harvard University was surveyed regarding their personal goals. Predictably, the class responded: money, power, and reputation—in that order. Doubtless they were simply reflecting the prevailing mood of university students throughout North America.[13] It's no surprise! Their parents are the baby boomers, who probably constitute the most self-centered, self-serving generation ever produced in American culture. In their pursuit of money, power, and reputation they are simply echoing the values of their parents into the next generation.

"The conductor of a great symphony orchestra was once asked which was the most difficult instrument to play. 'The second violin,' he answered. 'I can get plenty of first violinists, but to find someone who can play second violin with enthusiasm—that is a problem. And if we have no second violin, we have no harmony.'"[14] All of God's servants are second fiddles because all of them are subordinate to Jesus Christ. Our failure to recognize this, therefore giving only token acknowledgement to Christ's lordship, has produced massive disharmony in many ministry contexts.

There is no doubt that serving others is out; serving self is in. Even within the realm of ministry, the model for Christian service has become that of a corporation executive rather than that of a humble servant. The CEO syndrome has invaded the New Testament church. While management models from the business world may help us in becoming *efficient* at what we do in ministry, it's only a whole-hearted embracing of the servant model of Jesus Christ that will enable us to become *effective* at what we do in ministry. Efficient managers master routines, but effective leaders impact lives. "Managers are people who do things right and leaders are people who do the right thing."[15]

And what is the right thing when it comes to Christian ministry? Clearly, the right thing for Christian leaders is to think their way back into the historical and cultural milieu of first century Palestine, and especially into the heart and mind of Jesus Christ, finding out precisely what kind of a leader He was and then purposing to follow His example. I believe that we shall discover that to be Christ-like is to be servant-like. There's no room in Christian ministry for the pampered and the self-indulgent. "The towel and the basin, not pomp and power, are the symbols of redemptive ministry. The Cross, accepting suffering as the heart of God, not the computer, rejecting pain because it cannot be quantified and controlled, is the symbol of the servant leader."[16]

Qualities of a Servant Leader

If we are going to think our way back into the historical experience and personal ethic of Jesus of Nazareth with regard to this matter of servant leadership, perhaps the best place to look is Philippians 2:5-8. Without doubt this is one of the most astounding affirmations in Scripture of the deity, the humanity and the humility of Jesus Christ. In it are unfolded *five marvelous qualities* of a servant leader, which, if properly understood and implemented, will enable us to become effective leaders who impact lives for Jesus Christ. These are qualities, Paul says, which represent both Christ's way of thinking (v. 5) and His way of living (vv. 6-8). And he urges us to adopt both His philosophical perspective and its practical manifestation.

Servant Leaders Do Not Seek Status

First, servant leaders *selflessly repudiate status seeking*—"*Who, being in the form of God, thought it not robbery to be equal with God: But made Himself of no reputation . . .*" (2:6,7a). In these words Paul unveils three stages in Christ's life which together clearly demonstrate His antipathy for status seeking.

The first stage may be defined as *Christ's sovereign character* and is expressed in the words: "*Who, being in the form of God . . .*" A stronger, more profound statement of Christ's deity could not be imagined. There are two key words here which unmistakably identify Christ as God. The first word is "being." This is not a customary form of the simple verb "to be." It is a participial form of the special verb *huparchein* which means, "to be" or "to exist." It describes what a person is in his very essence and that which cannot be changed.[17] In His unchangeable essence, His "pretemporal existence,"[18] Jesus is God! *Huparchein* emphasizes the "continuance of an antecedent state or condition."[19] What He was in the eternal state, He continued to be in the temporal world. The second key word in this statement is "form" *(morphe)*, and *morphe* is the word which means "essential form which never alters."[20] Together these words make very clear who it is that is modeling servant leadership for us. It is the One who in His very essence is inalterably, unchangeably, immutably God! Talk about a legitimate claim to status! If anybody ever deserved it, it was Jesus Christ, but He is the only One who ever truly renounced it.

Stage two in Paul's revelation of Christ in this opening stanza is, *Christ's selfless consideration* which is expressed in the words: "*thought it not robbery to be equal with God.*" This is a difficult phrase, but what it actually means is that Christ did not consider equality with God something to be selfishly grasped. The Greek for "robbery" *(harpagmos)* means seizing selfishly, snatching violently, clutching greedily. In this word there is potential for great selfishness. This is precisely what Jesus was not. He was not selfish. After thoughtful consideration He was prepared to lay aside the glory, dignity and authority associated with His deity. He did not jealously cling to the powers and prerogatives which were rightfully His as God. Instead, He gave them up in the interests of the Father's will and our welfare. We can only imagine what a painful consideration this must have been. All true servants of God will have to be equally selfless.

Paul's third stage in the unveiling of Christ as the One who repudiates status-seeking is *Christ's sacrificial choice,* expressed in the words: *"But made Himself of no reputation."* Literally, Paul's phrase means that Christ emptied himself. The verb is *kenoo,* and it is a word which was used of pouring a liquid from a container until it was completely empty. Jesus Christ poured Himself empty in order to fill us full. Of what was Jesus emptied? His deity? Impossible! God can never cease to be God. It was not a *reduction* of deity but a *restraint* of it.[21] Jesus laid aside the insignia of deity; its distinguishing marks, badges and emblems; the visible indicators of His greatness and of His "Godness." He didn't forfeit the attributes and powers of deity, but the appearances and privileges of deity. While He retained all the properties of deity, in the incarnation He refused to exercise them independently of the Father's will and the Spirit's working. "The *kenosis* was this act of self-abnegation in which His native glory which He had enjoyed from all eternity (John 17:5,24) was hidden in His becoming man."[22] What this means is that Jesus was not interested in either status seeking (He refused to selfishly clutch to Himself the status symbols.) or kingdom building (He poured Himself empty; made Himself nothing; gave up His reputation; and entered poverty to make us wealthy.). Elitists and kings never do such things; servant leaders always do!

But aren't these the very things that we are so interested in? Our own status? Our own kingdoms? We want so much to be distinguished; we want high visibility, i.e., we want to be seen, to be noticed, even to be applauded! What is our rank in the hierarchy of authority? Do others see it, know it, applaud it? If not, we will help them! How unlike our Model we are. All of this is self and we are called to a radical manifestation of unself! The *kenosis* teaches us that self is something to be poured out. But we do it for a different reason than Christ. He poured out His sinless self to redeem sinful men; we pour out our sinful self to glorify a holy God and serve a needy race. His was an act of undeserved generosity; ours is an act of *"reasonable service"* (Romans 12:1-2). Appearances and privileges meant little to Him. Sometimes they mean everything to us. It is too often true that contemporary ministry has dipped to the level of status seeking and kingdom building. Authentic ministry will have none of it!

Servant Leaders Serve Voluntarily

The second marvelous quality of a servant leader may be defined as follows: servant leaders *humbly embrace bond-serving—"And took upon Him the form of a servant"* (Philippians 2:7b). The first and most immediate result of Christ's self-emptying was servant living. It naturally follows. Preoccupation with status effectively eliminates service; repudiation of status immediately initiates service.

Paul's word for servant is *doulos* and means literally "slave." It describes someone who is bound or in bondage (from *deo*, to bind). It was the term which described the lowest level in the hierarchy of servitude and came also to describe one who gives himself up to the will of another.[23] Bond-slaves have no property, time, rights, or will of their own. It was "a term of extreme abasement, the exact opposite of *kurios* (Lord), a title that later is used to describe the exalted Christ."[24] And it must be remembered that Paul once again uses the word *morphe* (form). It means that Jesus was not play acting nor was He wearing a mask. He was not superficially a servant, but essentially a servant; His servitude was not artificial, but authentic. In fact, it was sacrificial service which defined the very purpose of the incarnation (Mark 10:45).

Les Ollila, the president of the college where I teach, has often defined contemporary leaders as "bigshots in a hurry." He sees so many of them showing up late to meetings at which they speak and leaving early because they are either too busy or too important to deal with individual needs. They seem to be more interested in platforms than in people; in visibility than humility. But their patronizing smiles and waves from a distance can never become a substitute for immediate and personal involvement and investment in the lives of needy people. Jesus Christ was not a platform person, but a people person. And it was His servant living which graphically demonstrated this truth!

It may be that the material in Philippians 2:5-11 is shaped by one powerful event in the life of Christ which had at its heart the concept of abject servitude. That event was, of course, His washing of the disciples' feet (John 13:3-17). It is possible that Paul's material in Philippians is shaped in such a way as to match with his reflections on that astounding behavior of Christ. "The parallels in thought and in this progression of action are startling. So precise in fact are these parallels that it is difficult to consider them the result of mere coincidence. To present this parallelism more clearly the diagram on the following page has been prepared."[25]

Without doubt this was an electrifying moment for each of the disciples. "The Midrash taught that no Hebrew, even a slave, could be commanded to wash feet."[26] But that is precisely what Jesus had done. The sovereign of the universe had become the slave of the disciples. And what He did He expects us to do (John 13:13-16). And if we comply by performing humble acts for those in need (foot-washing being one example of such serving in the first century), then we can expect a special blessing from the Lord (13:17).

This can only mean that actual, fleshed-out deeds of menial service in behalf of others are not only appropriate, but requisite for all of God's servants, no matter their station in life. Philippians 2 is the theoretical/theological proposition which

John 13:3-17	Philippians 2:5-11
Jesus arises and lays aside His outer garments (v. 4).	He emptied Himself; laid aside His divine glory (His "outer garments" or the visible manifestation of His deity) (v. 7).
He takes a towel and wraps it about Himself, puts water in a basin and washes the disciples' feet — a menial task assigned to slaves (I Samuel 25:41) (v. 5).	He takes the form of a slave, being born in human likeness and then humbling Himself (v. 7).
When finished, He once again takes His outer garments and puts them back on. He again sits down at the table from which He got up (v. 12).	Therefore, God highly exalted Him and gave Him the name above every name (v. 9).
Finally, Jesus says: "ye call me Master and Lord *(kurios)* : and ye say well; for so I am" (v. 13).	And Paul says: "that every tongue should confess that Jesus Christ is Lord *(kurios)* to the glory of God the Father" (v. 11).

supports this thesis and John 13 is the functional/practical performance. Both are essential. Theory without practice is hypocrisy. Practice without theory leads to heresy.

If we have reached a point where we can say: "This or that person or work is beneath my dignity," which implies that we are somehow above theirs, then we have ceased being servant leaders and have become power seekers. Authentic servants of God must be open to, and periodically involved in, the performance of menial tasks. We need such humbling assignments in order to combat the crushing bondage of ego which confronts all of us on a daily basis. Servant leaders, then, are people who repudiate status-seeking and embrace bond-serving.

Servant Leaders Love Meeting People's Needs

Thirdly, servant leaders *warmly cherish need-meeting*, and this is a concept which is expressed in the words: *"and was made in the likeness of men"* (2:7c). What do these words have to do with need-meeting? Everything! The purpose of the incarnation, God made flesh, was the glorification of the Father through the liberation of man. It was God's bridge thrown across the chasm separating Him in His holiness from us in our sinfulness.

The language is graphic. *Made* is from a Greek verb which stresses "beginning or becoming." Christ always existed *"in the form of God,"* but He came into existence *"in the likeness of men."*[27] One, He had always natively been; the other, He voluntarily became.

This is a very costly procedure. Dust was added to deity, the word was made flesh, the divine Son became a Jewish carpenter, the Almighty appeared on earth as a helpless, wriggling and utterly dependent baby when the eternal God became a human being! The human babyhood of the divine Godhead is a staggering mystery; a reality eclipsing fantasy and a fact far exceeding fiction.

Why did He bother to enter our world, identify with our race, and die for our sins? Because He saw desperate needs and felt compelled to meet them (Luke 19:10).

He came where we are (John 17:18). Have we ever felt the compulsion to go where the needy are? Or have we found it easier to hide-out in our holy huddles or remain bottled-up in our elegant little ecclesiastical salt-shakers?

He was made flesh (John 1:14). We, too, are responsible to flesh out the gospel ethic and tell forth the gospel message. At the heart of the gospel is death, burial, and resurrection (I Corinthians 15:1-4). For that ethic to be fleshed out in our lives there will have to be a personification of a death to self-centeredness and a resurrection to unself-centeredness. For that message to be forth told by us there will have to be an affirmation of the good news of Christ's death *"for our offenses"* and of His resurrection *"for our justification"* (Romans 4:25).

He dwelt among us (John 1:14). Are we ever rubbing shoulders with the lost and mingling with riffraff (publicans, sinners, prostitutes, and lepers)? Jesus did! Like Him, we should be finding out their needs and meeting them; inviting them into our homes and befriending them; seeking to understand their viewpoints and lifestyles and ministering to them Biblically.

Are we entering their world like Christ through the incarnation entered our world? He was made in our likeness. Why? So that in human likeness He could face the human predicament experientially and meet human needs sacrificially.

Servant Leaders Humble Themselves

The fourth marvelous quality of a servant leader may be defined in the following terms: servant leaders *genuinely practice self-humbling*—*"And being found in fashion as a man, he humbled himself and became obedient . . ."* (2:8a).

This self-humbling of Jesus Christ includes the whole circumference of His life, from His incarnation or birth in the manger where He was *"made flesh"* and took on Himself our humanness to His crucifixion or death on the cross where He was *"made sin"* and *"made a curse"* and took on Himself our sinfulness. From beginning to end, one humble word characterized the entirety of Christ's life, a word which expresses the essential nature and fruit of His humility: it is the word *obedience.*

Obedience (hupakouo) is a humble word. In Greek it is so constructed as to mean "to listen under" or "to listen submissively" and thus "to listen obediently." At the heart of self-humbling is submissive obeying. That is always the visible evidence of an authentic, humble spirit for in all true obedience there is submission and in all true submission there is humility.

Although obedience is a regular theme of Pauline theology he uses this term of Jesus Christ only one other time in Romans 5:19: *"For as by one man's disobedience many were made sinners, so by the obedience of one shall many be made righteous."* In this passage the obedience of Christ is contrasted with the disobedience of Adam. Paul's word for disobedience is *parakouo*, which means "to listen alongside" as though we were God's peer, His equal! By definition it means the refusal to listen to God's voice, to His revealed will. Adam, who was natively humanity, aspired to deity *("ye shall be as gods")* by exalting himself and refusing obedience to the divine will. Christ who was natively deity assumed humanity *("the Word was made flesh")* by humbling himself and welcoming obedience to the divine will. On which side of that equation do we find ourselves? Are we Adamlike or Christlike?

On a functional basis, it means that all authentic servants of God know their place and gladly take it. And what is our place? On our faces before Jesus Christ exalting His name and kingdom, not on our "thrones" before the watching world exalting our own name and kingdom. This is the true destiny of a slave *(doulos)* before his Lord *(Kurios)*. "He has no choice but to obey his master . . . . At all points he stands in contrast to the master, the *kurios*."[28] All genuine servants of the Most High God welcome this privilege of investing their lives in the fulfillment of the will of another and assuming their position as obedient and humble subordinates. They genuinely practice self-humbling.

Servant Leaders Accept Cross-bearing

Finally, Paul suggests that servant leaders *bravely endure cross-bearing—"And became obedient unto death, even the death of the cross."*

We have seen already that Christ was obedient. Now we must see that His obedience was *no ordinary obedience.* It was an obedience unto death. In place of the customary preposition *eis* (unto), Paul uses the Greek particle *mechri* : which means "as far as . . . to the point of"[29] and carries the connotation of "all the way unto." It accentuates the absoluteness, the extremity of Christ's obedience. It was an obedience all the way unto death.

But Paul is not finished. If Christ's obedience is no ordinary obedience because it leads all the way to death, then Christ's death is *no ordinary death* because it leads all the way to the cross! The word "cross" in Paul's sentence is *anarthrous* (without the definite article). What this does is accentuate the quality of whatever is being addressed. In this case, Christ's death—it was a cross death! It was a death marked by intense suffering and intense shame; a death which was reserved exclusively for rebels, runaway slaves, raw criminals—the riffraff of the Roman Empire! Neither Paul, who was a Roman citizen, nor the Christians of Philippi, which was a Roman colony, could ever be subjected to crucifixion, but Jesus of Nazareth was!

And the wonder of Christ's cross death is that it is for others. There was a vicarious or substitutive intent attached to it (I Peter 2:24; 3:18). All cross-bearing, all redemptive living, whether we are talking about Christ's great cross or our little ones (Luke 9:23) is others oriented. It is a call to sacrificial investment in the well-being of another.

It can only mean that true servants of God endure sacrifice rather than run from it. They are prepared to sacrifice money, time, comfort, ease, popularity, position, power, selfish plans, and personal aspirations in order to serve God by serving others for His glory and their good. Only then can we lay claim to the title "Authentic Servant" because the shape of all true Christian service is what somebody has called "cruciform." That is, Christian service always demands Christian sacrifice, and the form that sacrifice takes is crucifixion of self for the benefit of others. Servant leaders accept cross-bearing as a part of normal life.

How then do servant leaders actually lead? In their repudiation of power seeking and their embracing of servant leading, are they somehow reducing themselves to the status of wimps or emptying themselves of the authority which is necessary to lead? I think not! While whole books have been written on the mechanisms of leadership, let me make two simple suggestions which may bring into focus how servant leaders lead.

How Servant Leaders Lead

They Lead by Feeding, Not Beating

The connection between feeding and leading is apparent in several key passages of the New Testament. For example, I Thessalonians 5:12 says : *"And we beseech you brethren, to know them which labor among you, and are over you in the Lord, and admonish you."* Those who are "over you" (i.e., who take the lead) are the same ones who "admonish you." They lead by feeding! I Peter 5:2 makes the same connection: *"feed the flock of God . . . taking the oversight thereof . . . ."* Christian sheep who are consistently well fed by the shepherd will gladly follow their shepherd's Biblical leadership (cf. Hebrews 13:7).

They Lead by Moral Example, Not Verbal Decree

It is Peter who once again addresses this issue in I Peter 5:2 and 3 where he teaches us that pastoral leadership *("taking the oversight thereof")* is not to be ritualistic—*"not by constraint,"* nor materialistic—*"not for filthy lucre,"* nor is it to be despotic—*"neither as being lords over God's heritage."* Those who lord it over (the same brutalizing term which Jesus forbids in Matthew 20:25-26) the flock are those who enjoy ruling by fiat, by ordering people about and expecting that others should bow whenever they "bark." But Peter insists that this is not God's way of leadership. In echoing what he had learned from Jesus, he calls us to lead by moral example—*"being ensamples to the flock."* There is a moral magnetism attached to the right kind of example. In such magnetism the compulsion to follow comes from internal rather than external constraints, and the exercise of the believer-priest's will is authentic rather than plastic.

It seems to me that the function of leadership is to get people to follow, and both Peter and Paul seem to be suggesting that this is better accomplished by feeding and modeling than by beating or commanding.

This does not discount the occasional necessity of what I have come to call pastoral prerogatives. A "prerogative" may be defined as, "a right or privilege attached to an office or rank." There are times when a pastor must exercise God-given authority in a specific situation without being able to link his views to a specific passage of Scripture, but simply as a manifestation of prudence (Proverbs 27:12). An occasional (not an habitual) exercise of this nature, which is grounded in a Biblical principle, if not a specific Biblical passage, is acceptable to spiritually-minded people, who sense their God-given responsibility to the kind of spiritual leadership which seeks to both nourish the body and model the truth. However, servant leaders studiously avoid making their people the prisoners of their pastoral prerogatives by exercising them habitually.

So the true servants of God are those who are acutely aware of the dynamics of power and have taken specific steps to protect themselves from its corruptive influence. In addition, they have decided against being heavy-handed, manipulative dictators and, instead, have chosen to be humble-minded, Christlike servants. Such a choice requires of them a reduplication in the modern world of the mind of Christ. This will mean, as we have seen, that they strive to become servant leaders who in very practical ways share Christ's attitude toward status-seeking, bond-serving, need-meeting, self-humbling and cross-bearing. In this way they are powerfully equipped to feed God's flock and model God's truth! Such feeders and examples are leaders *par excellence!*

CHAPTER THREE

REDISCOVERING AUTHENTIC EVANGELISM

"Their clear and precise understanding of the appalling need and tragic plight of unregenerate man moved both Jesus Christ and the New Testament believers to make a sacrificial investment of their lives in behalf of others. What does it do for us? How has it moved us and where has it sent us?"

Ben-hadad and the Syrian army laid siege to the ancient city of Samaria in the ninth century B.C. When it seemed that all was lost and the city was near to death by starvation, God supernaturally intervened and routed the Syrian army leaving their camp emptied of soldiers but filled with food. Certain starving lepers, who earlier had been expelled from the city of Samaria because of their leprous condition, stumbled on these vast resources of an entire army. Predictably, they began to engage in one of our modern habits of hoarding, hugging, and hiding riches until they remembered the starving souls in the city of Samaria who were completely oblivious to this bounty. Then, in response to a quickened conscience, they very wisely said to one another: *"We do not well: this day is a day of good tidings, and we hold our peace . . ."* (II Kings 7:9). Quite literally the Hebrew reads emphatically: "Not right!" What was not right? Their selfish hoarding of resources which were meant by God not only to benefit them, but also others; their inexcusable silence after having been endowed with a life-giving discovery. Their consciences were smitten. We who know the life-giving message and fail to share it are equally guilty.

Mission agencies are facing a crisis of personnel due to our "secular self-interest."[1] Within the next few years, before the year 2000, some 50% of the existing missionary force will retire. Who is going to replace them? Though figures differ, in general, mission agencies tell us that about 20,000 missionaries are preparing for retirement. Only 5,000 recruits are preparing to take their place. It doesn't take a mathematical genius to know that we are falling far behind the necessary pace to achieve global evangelism. And global evangelism is the business of every New Testament church. The Great Commission requires of us a vision and a strategy which demand local (Jerusalem), regional (Judea), cross-cultural (Samaria) and international (uttermost part of the earth) involvement (Acts 1:8, Mark 16:15). Clearly, we must find ways of rediscovering and reinstituting urgent, Biblical evangelism in contemporary fundamental churches!

The Nature of Evangelism

Evangelism is a ministry of reconciliation in a world of alienation. "To evangelize is so to present Jesus Christ in the power of the Holy Spirit that men come to put their faith in God through him, to accept him as their Savior and to serve him as their King in the fellowship of his Church."[2] Or, as someone put it more simply: "Evangelism is one beggar sharing with another beggar where to find bread."

If this is what evangelism is, who is supposed to do it? Clearly the New Testament command is not just for the paid professionals. New Testament evangelism focuses on the participation of every man, woman, and child. Our task is to mobilize once again the entire church so that its individual members will be renewed in their commitment to the evangelistic process and find their place in it. Kenneth Scott Latourette, renowned church historian, assigned the early expansion of primitive Christianity to the common laborers as opposed to the official leaders of the congregation. It was his judgment that "the chief agents in the expansion of Christianity appear not to have been those who made it a profession or made it a major part of their occupation, but men and women who carried on their livelihood in some purely secular manner and spoke of their faith to those they met in this natural fashion."[3] This can only mean that Biblical Fundamentalism needs a core of pastors who don't feel the necessity to jealously guard all ministry for themselves, but who feel the liberty to selflessly equip the saints to perform *"the work of the ministry"* (Ephesians 4:11,12). In this way the godly pastor, "instead of monopolizing all ministry himself . . . actually multiplies ministries."[4]

If the Gospel is the good news that it purports to be, and if the world is in the state of desperation that it appears to be, then it is absolutely essential that we, the people of God, and every single one of us, not just the paid professionals, become the Christian witnesses that God has called us to be. How can we overcome our self-centered fears and our self-protective silence? How can we "prime the pump" so that evangelism begins to flow out of us naturally? In this chapter I want to bring into focus *two monumental necessities* which must be fulfilled, if we ever intend to honor the evangelistic mandate which Jesus left us: recognizing the stifling factors, and rekindling the Spirit's fire.

When Jesus Christ walked on this globe there was a world population of about 250 million people. Today over 5 billion people are crowded into the same space and by the year 2000 the figure will be 6 billion. That translates into a population growth on planet earth of approximately 85-90 million people annually, 250,000 daily and 10,000-plus hourly. Such figures create not simply a staggering economic problem for the governments of this world, but, supremely, a sobering evangelistic problem for the Christians of this world. And this is a concern which Jesus felt for He said: *"The harvest truly is plenteous but the laborers are few"* (Matthew 9:37). What are we going to do about this awesome task of world evangelization? Obviously no one of us can reach the entire world, but each one of us can reach our own world—the world into which we go daily, the world of our neighborhood and family of the work place and the market place. But if we are going to do so effectively, we shall have to renounce our infection of apathy and recover our sense of urgency. How can we do this?

Recognizing the Stifling Factors

What is it that creates apathy and dissipates urgency? I believe there are at least three factors which account for the suffocation of evangelism in much of contemporary Christianity.

Pervasive Materialism

Materialism is no respecter of persons. In spite of the profound teachings of the Lord Jesus on the subject of finances, it wasn't very long before the New Testament Christians were facing their own personal struggles with either the hunger for money, if they didn't have it, or the wisdom to handle it, if they did. And this struggle was common both in the pulpit and the pew. The warnings to both groups in a number of the epistles make this abundantly clear (e.g. James 2:1-7; 4:13-17; I John 2:15-17; 3:17-18; I Peter 5:2-3; I Timothy 3:3; 6:6-10; 17-19).

And what proved to be a struggle in antiquity continues to be one today. For the first time in church history a majority of God's people are no longer on the outside looking in at the world's wealth; they are on the inside luxuriating in the world's wealth. The toys of the pagans and the toys of the Christians are essentially the same. In my opinion, this has taken its toll by dulling the keen edge of our spiritual vitality. We no longer rejoice in the Lord because we're too busy rejoicing in the things which money can buy.

It seems to me that evangelism and materialism cannot co-exist—they are completely incompatible. Why is that? Because evangelism is utterly sacrificial, whereas materialism is thoroughly preservational. They represent two wholly opposite world views. One has God at the center and is characterized by a loyal life of tough-going self-sacrifice in which "God and others first" is the watchword. The other has self at the center and is characterized by a lax life of easy-going self-indulgence in which "me first" is the watchword. Whenever you are preoccupied with your material self, it naturally follows that you will have no concern for the spiritual state of others.

Like Judas, many contemporary materialists are prepared to betray Jesus Christ, if the price is right (Matthew 26:15). So, Jesus in His personal manifesto, the Sermon on the Mount, in very vivid language warns us against the seductions of the wealth of this world by identifying for us its four grave dangers (Matthew 6:19-24).

The wealth of this world is cursed with transience (6:19-20)
Jesus is very clear: treasures on earth decay; treasures in heaven abide. Whatever is transient is always smitten with two great liabilities: it doesn't last and it doesn't satisfy. Malcom Muggeridge, as an octogenarian, in a retrospective moment confirms this:

> When I look back on my life nowadays . . . what strikes me most forcibly about it is that what seemed at the time most significant and seductive, seems now most futile and absurd. For instance, success in all of its various guises; being known and being praised; ostensible pleasures, like acquiring money or travelling, going to and fro in the world and up and down in it like Satan, explaining and experiencing whatever Vanity Fair has to offer.
>
> In retrospect, all these exercises in self-gratification seem pure fantasy, what Pascal called, "licking the earth."[5]

I wonder how many New Testament Christians squander their lives in "licking the earth" rather than investing them by "laying up treasures in heaven" where things both last and satisfy?

The wealth of this world captures the heart (6:21)
Human hearts are always tethered to human treasures. Our heart always follows our treasure whether up to heaven or

down to earth. Our treasures actually govern our lives because they control our heart, which is nothing less than the master control of life—the center of our person, the source of our problems and the focal point of our potential (Proverbs 4:23).

We may be "in Christ" judicially but since our treasure is not there functionally, neither is our heart. The tragic result is apathy regarding spiritual matters. We attend a Bible study and yawn; we go to church and fall asleep; we hear an impassioned appeal for help in ministry and outreach and remain untouched and unmoved. Why? What is the reason for our sense of detachment, distance, and disinterest in spiritual things? Simply stated, the reason is that we do not treasure spiritual things; we treasure material things. And *"where your treasure is, there will your heart be also."* What many of us need is a revival of authentic spiritual values which will move us to impute supreme value to and invest significant and sacrificial energy in the things of God. Then our hearts will be aflame for Christ and His work because they will be affixed to the right treasure. We take, too often, the best of what we are and have and invest it in the worst of treasurers. No wonder our hearts are so far afield!

The wealth of this world darkens the mind (6:22-23)

In the nomenclature of Scripture, the "single eye" is the generous eye. It describes those who give generously to the cause of Christ and the needs of others. That is how *haplous* (single) is used throughout the New Testament (cf. Romans 12:8; II Corinthians 8:2; 9:11,13; James 1:5). Conversely, the evil eye is the greedy or grudging eye, the selfish or miserly eye. That is how *poneros* (evil) is used, for example, in the Septuagint translation of the Old Testament (cf. Deuteronomy 15:9; Proverbs 23:6; 28:22).

Uniquely, we learn from these verses that generosity and mercy fill a person with light, but that greed and materialism fill a person with darkness. Why is that? To be generous and merciful is to be God-like. And what is God like? *"God is light and in Him is no darkness at all"* (I John 1:5). But to be greedy and materialistic is to be Satan-like. And what is Satan like? He is the prince of darkness and he rules the domain of darkness (Ephesians 2:2; 6:12; Colossians 1:13).

So people who go through life as takers instead of givers are bound to become like Satan instead of like God and their minds and manners will be flooded with darkness instead of light for Satan is the prince of darkness, whereas God is the fount of light. There can be no doubt, greed darkens the mind by excluding God and His word and by exploiting men and their needs. Materialists descend into the abyss of darkness, thinking dark, sinister, and self-serving thoughts and engaging in the same kinds of actions. Indisputably, evangelism perishes in the midst of such "Christian" darkness!

The wealth of this world enslaves to the wrong master (6:24)

Mammon is Hebrew for material possessions. The word had an innocent beginning but an idolatrous ending, for it came to stand for "that in which a person puts his trust."[6] It is perfectly proper to have material possessions in moderation, but it is never proper to place one's trust in them as though they can meet fundamental needs for it is obvious that they cannot (cf. Proverbs 23:4-5; 11:4,28).

The imagery behind Jesus' teaching in this verse is that of slave and slave owner. *Doulos* describes abject slavery; *Kurios* describes absolute ownership. While it is possible for a man to work for two employers, it is not possible to be the slave (or property) of two masters (or owners). The trouble with mammon is not that we own it, but that it all too often owns us. It becomes our *kurios* and we become its *doulos*. We begin spelling it with a capital "M" and regarding it as nothing less than a god. E. Calvin Beisner was right to say in *Discipleship Journal*:

> Ultimately worshipping mammon means worshipping self. For we covet wealth not for its own sake, but for our benefit. And that perspective betrays a broader and deeper attitude:

> everything, we think, exists to serve us. Thus we
> put ourselves in the place of God . . . What this
> means is that to worship mammon means to
> worship "me."[7]

It fits perfectly with the "me-first-ism" of the secular society, but
it is utterly incompatible with the Christian ethic.

Nothing has been more destructive of authentic, Biblical
evangelism than the materialistic appetites of those who are
supposed to do it. Those of us who have been infected with such
pervasive materialism shall have to open wide our eyes to the
teachings of Jesus on this subject and then open wide our hearts
to His call to repentance, revival, and the recovery of urgency in
evangelism!

Excessive Calvinism

The second stifling factor, which has contributed to the
suffocation of evangelistic zeal in our churches today is an
excessive Calvinism. Without doubt, the matter of God's
sovereignty and man's responsibility has boggled theologians
from the beginning of time. Anyone who thinks he has all of the
answers on this matter simply has not yet heard all of the
questions!

It is undeniably true that divine election is a teaching of
the Word of God (Ephesians 1:4; John 15:16; Acts 13:48; I
Thessalonians 1:4). It is not a fantasy of man: it is a mystery of
God. Since Scripture declines to explain the mystery, we must be
cautious about dogmatizing our particular view of this very
difficult issue.

Conversely, it is undeniably true that somehow, within
the circle of divine sovereignty, God has granted to His image-
bearers an authentic exercise of their wills (Matthew 23:37; Acts
7:51; II Peter 3:9,15; Romans 10:13). They are responsible
creatures who will be held accountable by their Creator. This can
only mean that there is in the matter of personal salvation an
inscrutable synergism, a mysterious working together of the

divine and human wills. For my part, I have been content to say that God has devised a plan which insures the fulfillment of the divine will without intersecting the integrity of the human will. Doubtless, it is only omniscience which could devise such a plan. Perhaps that is why we mere mortals find it so baffling. Richard Halverson put it this way: "Nothing God planned interferes with human freedom . . . . Nothing humans do frustrates God's sovereign plan!"[8]

What I know and understand about God's integrity gives me confidence regarding what I don't know or understand about God's sovereignty (cf. Genesis 18:25). Our ignorance of His ways is never a justification for either pessimism, cynicism, or criticism of His ways. What we need with respect to the matter of divine sovereignty and human responsibility is a Biblical balance. We need the honesty to acknowledge the existence of both sides of this theological equation and the humility to acknowledge our ignorance of exactly how they can be reconciled. Perhaps Spurgeon was correct to say, when asked how to reconcile these two truths, "I wouldn't try. I never reconcile friends." Neither Calvinism nor Arminianism will do, for both tend to be reasonable or logical systems. And the trouble with what is reasonable or logical is that it is not always Biblical or theological. There is the tendency to go beyond what Scripture says, or to radically reinterpret certain sections of it in order to make it fit one's preconceived system. Church historian, Philip Schaff calls for moderation and balance:

> Calvinism emphasizes divine sovereignty and free grace; Arminianism emphasizes human responsibility. The one restricts the saving grace to the elect; the other extends it to all men on the condition of faith. Both are right in what they assert; both are wrong in what they deny. If one important truth is pressed to the exclusion of another of equal importance, it becomes an error, and loses its hold upon the conscience. The

Bible gives us a theology which is more human
than Calvinism and more divine than
Arminianism, and more Christian than either of
them.[9]

My personal attempt to document this balance is
presented in the following chart:

Categories:	GOD'S SOVEREIGNTY		MAN'S RESPONSIBILITY
Views:	CALVINISM:	BIBLICISM:	ARMINIANISM:
Emphasis:	Strong emphasis on sovereign will of God	Acceptance of an inscrutable synergism—will of God working with will of man.	Strong emphasis on free will of man.
Effect:	Overemphasis here tends to fatalism and dead ritualism	Two-fold Effect: 1. Quiet Confidence because God is at work. 2. Energetic Activity because God has commanded man to be at work.	Overemphasis here tends to fear/frustration and defective emotionalism.

It is not difficult to see how one's view of these issues
could radically impact his view of evangelism. An excessive
Calvinism almost always ends in a dead fatalism. People grow
stoic, Islamic ("Allah wills it!") and apathetic. God's servants
begin to excuse their personal responsibility on the basis of an
eccentric and unbalanced view of divine sovereignty. Among
other things, this constitutes a failure to see that a sovereign God
is free to ordain not only the end but the means. And in the
matter of evangelism, the means is urgent Christian witness by all
the members of the body of Christ.

But the opposite is equally true. If an excessive Calvinism terminates in a dead fatalism, then an excessive Arminianism terminates in a destructive fanaticism. People grow frantic and humanistic. The result in such contexts is the generating of a great deal of heat and very little light. If it is all in human hands, then whatever works becomes permissible. There develops a sort-of "salvatory humanism" which is nearly as dangerous as secular humanism. Humanism can invade even evangelism. You can always recognize this invasion because everything in evangelism then becomes psychological and sociological. Inevitably the Gospel is packaged and marketed almost as though it were a plastic toy.

For the authentic Christian witness neither stoic Calvinism nor its antonym, frantic Arminianism will do. Instead, a balanced biblicism must prevail. The authentic witness possesses, as we have already seen, a quiet confidence because he recognizes a divine sovereignty in which God is at work. And he is marked by an energetic activity because he acknowledges a human responsibility in which man is obedient to the divine command to be at work. This combination of confidence in God and investment in men, of balancing divine sovereignty with human responsibility will go a long way toward enabling us to recover urgency and authenticity in our evangelism. But an imbalance on either side of the equation will suffocate it.

Oppressive Fundamentalism

The third and final stifling factor in evangelism is an oppressive Fundamentalism. This is an oppression which takes the form of a status-quo rigidity vs. a Spirit-filled flexibility. Rigidity speaks of being tight fisted, bull headed or closed minded. It describes someone who is stubborn or obstinate and resists change. Flexibility speaks of being adjustable, adaptable, or alterable. It describes someone who is capable of being modified, open to influence, or responsive to changing conditions. In my mind there is a desperate need for flexibility when it comes to evangelistic methodology. This is a flexibility, of course, which has certain contingencies. It is not open ended but neither is it closed minded. We are speaking here only of Spirit-filled and Bible-based flexibility. But within that framework there is room for a great deal more modification than many fundamentalists have ever realized.

Hostility to Change

There has developed within certain segments of Fundamentalism a hostility to change, no matter its form or purpose. This kind of intransigence has grown out of a tendency to make non-absolutes into absolutes or to impute divine authority to human traditions.

Let me make clear that we are not advocating a ruthless abandonment of tried and true methods, but rather an openness to new and creative approaches to evangelism, so long as they fit within Biblical boundaries.

Change for the sake of change

It seems to me that there are two kinds of change. First, there is *pragmatic* change. That is change for change's sake! Its purpose is often accommodation or imitation of the world system, and it appears to encourage compromise for soteriological reasons—it is ready to concede or give away certain elements of God's truth if that will provide a broader base for evangelism. Anyone who is committed to the entirety of God's Word could never engage in such change.

Change for Christ's sake

The second kind of change is *principial* change. Its purpose is to increase both efficiency and effectiveness in genuine ministry and outreach. Far from encouraging compromise, it strongly resists it for doxological reasons. It recognizes the exaltation of God's name as the controlling factor in all that it does, including evangelism. The idea that it is legitimate to compromise one segment of God's truth in order to propagate another segment of God's truth is unthinkable to people who are committed to principled change.

Nor are we suggesting that the concept of tradition is intrinsically wrong. The right kind of tradition is very valuable. Traditions enable us to define roles, helping us to understand who we are and what we are to do. They provide stability and security within a community of believers, whereas senseless changes erode it. Moreover, the right kinds of traditions establish a basis for inter-generational bonding by providing an observable link with our forebears. All of this is good.

Traditionalism

However, that which has been most hurtful to urgent and effective evangelism within Fundamentalism is not tradition but traditionalism. Bill Hull gives a classic definition to these two terms which helps us to see how crippling to evangelism the wrong approach to tradition can be.

> *Tradition* is the living faith of godly progenitors, passed on from generation to generation. *Traditionalism* is the dead faith of living Christian leaders attempting to hold on to power . . . . Tradition is a good thing. Families, churches, clubs, businesses, all practice traditions that form foundations for corporate values. Churches need tradition, not only in doctrine, but in many familial practices. Tradition runs into trouble when it sours and becomes traditionalism.[10]

Do we dare face ourselves squarely? Some of us within Fundamentalism are practicing traditionalism. In our insistence that "my way is the only way," we have begun to shut down authentic ministry. Unwittingly, we have embraced a posture of resistance to the will and Word of God. It's no surprise. It happened in the Judaism of Jesus' day.

> *Then came to Jesus scribes and Pharisees, which*
> *were of Jerusalem, saying, Why do thy disciples*
> *transgress the tradition of the elders? for they*
> *wash not their hands when they eat bread. But*
> *he answered and said unto them, Why do ye also*
> *transgress the commandment of God by your*
> *tradition?* (Matthew 15:1-3)

Clearly, the will of God is in jeopardy when traditionalism takes
priority. Once again Hull adds a perceptive insight:

> As a result, [we can] hinder progress and create
> an atmosphere of conflict. The "founding
> fathers" of a particular church find themselves
> fighting to death over unimportant issues. Many
> times they forget the reason for the battle, and
> the conflict takes on a life of its own. Too often,
> the entire church dons full mountain-climbing
> gear to ascend anthills.[11]

Antiquated Methodology

What this means is that we need to begin not only living
in the modern world but actually ministering in it. Few of us are
driving Model-T's to church, but some of us are antiquated in our
methodology. Of course, innovative methodology alone is
inadequate to initiate authentic evangelism.   It must be
accompanied by a revival of Biblical values and theology. Then,
when innovation is used both "constructively and critically,
accompanied by a parallel reformation of truth and theology, the
potential for the gospel would be incalculable."[12] As we have said
earlier, it is possible to make adaptation in our methodology to
the culture without experiencing contamination by our culture.
And from my perspective, it is not only possible, it is absolutely
essential. Without it we will become ineffective in evangelism

and incapable of retaining the next generation of thinking pastors within the fundamentalist orbit.

Alternative Models of Evangelism

And what kind of adaptations are we recommending? How about encouraging personal evangelism in all the normal connections of life (friends, neighbors, fellow-workers, relatives) rather than tying it exclusively to a structured, one-night-a-week program. How about establishing a network of evangelistic Bible studies, under the auspices of the local church and directed at specific groups of need (women, singles, students, couples, etc.). How about developing a ministry of rehabilitation for drug addicts and alcoholics, a ministry which is thoroughly Christ-centered rather than generically theistic, a program which is grounded in Jesus Christ of Nazareth, not in "God as you perceive Him." How about targeting communities of brokenness in our world and developing strategies to reach them—street people, dislocated internationals (Hmongs, Southeast Asians, etc.), unwed mothers, prisoners, children in fractured and uncaring homes (a sensible and responsible bus ministry which ministers to the real needs of such children). How about implementing a series of "Hope Conferences" which target those who have experienced sexual abuse, financial reversals, terminal illness and grief, and broken families, and providing for them structured and Biblical resources which enable them to cope and conquer in the midst of despairing circumstances. How about organizing a crisis pregnancy center in your community with other churches of like faith and practice, a ministry which enables you to shine as light rather than merely to shout at the darkness, and which permits you to minister to the real needs of young mothers while at the same moment to rescue the lives of their unborn children. These are but a few of the adaptations which might be considered within a fundamentalist orbit. And I am certain that with some thoughtful meditation, all of us are capable of generating our own ideas regarding new and effective models of evangelism.

It is true that over the years we have tended to be more event oriented than strategy oriented. We have majored on evangelistic events on the church property rather than focusing on specific groups within our community and developing strategies to reach them. The result has been that we have become very ingrown in our perspective. We have relied on people coming to us rather than fulfilling the mandate to go to them with a strategy to win them. This is something which needs to change if we hope to keep pace with the exploding needs of a secular society.

I would suggest at least four basic guidelines in making our adaptations and developing our strategies:

1. Is there a real need?
2. Are the resources there (human, financial, facility)?
3. Can the Christian ethic, the Word of God, be honored?
4. Has the Holy Spirit prompted?

If, after much thought and careful study of the Word of God, the answer to all four questions is yes, then what could hold us back? When we face Jesus Christ at the *Bema*, the excuses of tradition or peer pressure won't wash! If we are to recover urgency in evangelism, we'll have to make the transition from the status-quo to Spirit-filled, Bible-based change.

If recognizing the stifling factors is the first necessity in recovering urgency in evangelism, what is the second?

Rekindling the Spirit's Fire

What must happen for this rekindling to take place? As I see it, there are two essential ingredients which must be factored into our lives if the flames of evangelism are once again to burn brightly in our personal and corporate ministries.

Biblical Prompting

First, we will need a Biblical prompting. What this means is that we need a right set of *motivations*. Over the past several decades the body of Christ has been guided by false and inadequate incentives when it comes to evangelism, and it stands in need of a whole new set of true and compelling incentives. We need to be cleansed of false motives and set aflame by true ones.

What are some of the false motives which have controlled evangelism and burned-out Christians over the past thirty years? There is the human success syndrome, which believes that "bigger is better" no matter the cost. There is the pacification of guilt feelings, which puts the accent on how I feel. There is the gaining of status in "the cult"—the promotion and admiration which come from our peers when we produce. And, finally, there is the hunger for personal empire building—the audacious belief that one can use gospel preaching and personal witnessing for building a circle of control. The trouble with all of these incentives is that at their core they are self-centered. This won't do for unself-centered ministry. Love of self is always the wrong starting point for evangelism. True evangelism is always preoccupied with love of souls.

Motives are critically important to ministry because God always looks at the heart to determine the value of the deed (Jeremiah 17:9-10). If our motives are self-centered, they will be torched at the *Bema*; they won't survive the fire test. So what is it that constitutes a right set of motives? What are the elements of the Biblical prompting which should impel us to evangelism?

Obedience to the Holy Scripture

Our first motivation is obedience to the Holy Scripture, especially to the Great Commission. First and foremost, we ought to be involved in Christian witness out of plain obedience to the divine mandate. We do it for no other reason than that God told us to do it and love always obeys (John 14:23,24). The servants of Christ are responsible to be obedient to Christ. They are always concerned to do His will and keep His commandments

—and that means all of them. We are not at liberty to pick and choose which we shall obey and which we shall ignore. Our obedience is to be total and it is to be comprehensive.

This is especially true of His final command—*"Go . . . and make disciples."* In each of the first five books of the New Testament we are given a record of Christ's universal commission to the Church. We are the recipients of one great mandate—evangelize! It is stated formally no less than five times, and on each occasion there is a little different nuance of emphasis.

In Matthew 28:18-20 we're given the strategy of our ministry. In a nutshell the strategy is evangelize, baptize, and teach (v. 19,20) relying upon Christ's unlimited power (v. 18) and His unending presence (v. 20). It is amazing what ordinary people can do when they know that an extraordinary God is with them!

In Mark 16:15 we're given the scope of our mission—*"All the world . . . every creature."* There are no geographical or racial boundaries to this mandate. God makes a rich offer and it is a universal offer. Everyone is included, no one is excluded.

In Luke 24:47 we're given the substance of our message—*"repentance and remission of sins."* From the very beginning we are taught that there must be a decisive break with sin (repentance) before there can be a divine cleansing from sin (remission). All true followers of Jesus Christ are prepared in principle to forsake all lesser loyalties. This is the message we are to proclaim.

In John 20:21 we're given the source of our mandate. It comes from Jesus Christ Himself, so it is impossible that we should ignore it.

In Acts 1:8 we're given the strength of our manpower. Clearly, the energy for ministry is not in man himself, but in the Holy Spirit who has come to live within him. If He does not speak through us, then all of our witness will be utterly ineffectual (cf. John 15:26,27).

So we are taught from the lips of the Lord Jesus that we are bound by the universal commission to evangelize. And He doesn't say it only once but on repeated occasions so that it is difficult to miss. There is no room for doubt, disagreement, debate, or dodging our responsibility. He has laid squarely on our shoulders the proud privilege and the awesome responsibility of sharing in His ministry to humanity by engaging in Biblical evangelism. The New Testament Christians took Him seriously. Do we? One of the reasons for which they gave themselves so unremittingly to this task of global evangelism was that they took so seriously His final command: *"Go . . . teach . . . baptizing them . . . I am with you always."* They obeyed! Have we? Why should we get involved in evangelism? Why should we even bother? Because He told us to and love always obeys!

Love for the fallen sinner

But if obedience to the holy Scriptures is the first motivation to engage in evangelism, then surely love for the fallen sinner is the second. In this point I want to focus on two key concepts.

The condition of fallen sinners. It helps us to see how Jesus saw those to whom He ministered. Then perhaps we can understand a little better His sacrificial investment in their lives. In Luke 4:18 Jesus, in identifying the nature of His Messianic mission, tells us precisely how He saw people.

He saw them bankrupt—*"for He hath anointed me to preach the gospel to the poor."* It means that in evangelism we are dealing with the spiritually destitute. Not those who have nothing superfluous but those who have nothing at all! They are utterly incapable of helping themselves back to God. So it was Christ who came to help them.

He saw them broken—*"he hath sent me to heal the brokenhearted."* It means that in evangelism we are dealing with the emotionally shattered. As we close out what was supposed to have been a golden century it is apparent that it has turned into a tragic century—a broken world filled with deep-rooted despair and hopelessness. The fundamental cause of this is our detachment from God. When a man gives up God he is bound to give up hope. And the farther our culture drifts from God the greater will be our experience of despair. Already it is profoundly evident in art, which is the mirror of our age; in music, which is the voice of our age; in cinema, which is the imitation (and sometimes the manipulation) of our age; and in literature, which is the thought of our age. Jesus saw people broken and He responded to their need.

He saw them bound—"to preach deliverance to the captives." It means that in evangelism we are dealing with the morally conquered. It's a picture of people who are defeated and duped by a more powerful foe; a portrait of being confronted with and conquered by the world, the flesh, and the devil. They have high ideals but weak wills. They want to do right but they're always doing wrong. They find in themselves no source of recuperative energy by which to extricate themselves. But Jesus Christ remains the greatest liberator in the universe, and evangelism is affirming that truth and leading people to it, by leading them to Him!

He saw them blind—"and recovering of sight to the blind." It means that in evangelism we are dealing with the intellectually groping. Society's repudiation of the category of the absolute has left it with no reference point, no set of guidelines by which to live. In a world with no fixed axioms or moral absolutes, life becomes unbearable, intolerable, and unstable. To such people, who may even tend to become suicidal in the midst of such darkness, Jesus Christ is the light of the world, and He shines to them through us!

He saw them bruised—"to set at liberty them that are bruised." It means that in evangelism we are dealing with the mortally wounded. Bruised is the word which means crushed, broken in pieces. Jesus uses it to picture the total disintegration of humanity due to sin. Like Humpty Dumpty when he fell, humanity, too, is in a situation in which "all the king's horses and all the king's men couldn't put 'humanity' together again."

But Jesus Christ can! He puts shattered lives, fractured marriages, and broken families back together again. And evangelism is telling that message and pointing to that Christ.

This is how Jesus saw people, and when He did He was moved with compassion (Matthew 9:36). It was this knowledge of the condition of lost sinners which brought Jesus to earth in the incarnation and to the cross in the crucifixion. And it was this same knowledge which sent the apostles and the New Testament church to the ends of the earth in proclamation. Their clear and precise understanding of the appalling need and tragic plight of unregenerate man moved them to make a sacrificial investment of their lives in the behalf of others. What does it do for us? How has it moved us and where has it sent us?

The Character of Biblical Love. The second important concept, following the condition of lost sinners, is the character of biblical love. In the simplest of terms love possesses four great qualities.

It sees. Nothing which smacks of need escapes its attention. It is tragically true that it is possible to live out the entirety of our lives seeing without seeing. We can become so self-absorbed that we never see anything or anybody but self. That is the antithesis of love!

It feels. Like the heart of Christ, it is moved with compassion. The word that is thus translated in the New Testament documents is so powerful that it approximates the moral equivalent of a physical cardiac arrest. How long has it been since we felt intensely the needs of others?

It speaks. It speaks the word of comfort to the sorrowful, the word of peace to the troubled, the word of fullness to the empty, the word of hope to the despairing, the word of truth to the deceived, the word of love to the unlovely, and the word of salvation to the lost! Love knows what to speak, when to speak, and how to speak, and it does so with courage, clarity, and compassion.

It acts. Bill Hull warns of "Christians who are experts on what they are not experiencing."[13] Becoming masters of wordcraft will not do when it comes to this matter of Biblical love. We need fewer definitions of *agape* and more demonstrations of it. We must become practitioners who go beyond abstract wordcraft to concrete lifestyle. It is possible for us to be precise in our knowledge of a concept but inept in our implementation of it. Authentic Christianity won't stand for such hypocrisy. If we love Biblically we shall have to love practically. That can only mean that we will touch someone else with the gospel of Jesus Christ.

In Luke 7:11-17 you find every one of these qualities of love fleshed-out in the ministry of Jesus. When Jesus saw (love is *perceptive*) the funeral procession coming out from the city of Nain, bearing the body of a young man, the only son of a widowed mother, He was *"moved with compassion"* (love is *passionate*), and He *"said unto her, Weep not"* (love is *propositional*). And then He came and touched the coffin, restored that son to life and delivered him to his mother (love is *practical*). I love the verbs in this passage because verbs are words of action. They get things done! Verbs are the work horses; they're in the trenches unafraid to break sweat and to soil themselves and their clothing. Gerry Craig was right to teach us to pray: "Make me a verb, Lord. . . . Make me a strong verb." If Biblical love is to become a reality in our lives, we'll have to be practical. And the most profound verb, which both encapsulates and expresses the very essence of love, is the verb "to give." In fulfilling the mandate to evangelize, we shall have to give away not only our substance but ourselves in sacrificial and selfless investment in the well-being of others.

Dread of the Coming Sentence
So Christians must possess an obedient spirit—obedience to the holy Scriptures, and a compassionate spirit—love for the fallen sinner. But there is a third and sobering motivation to overcome our essential self-centeredness and sacrificially involve ourselves in evangelism. It is dread of the coming sentence, the awesome and dreadful implications of the holy wrath of God

coming down on the heads of fallen man. And this should supply us with an urgent spirit. It is important to see three alarming truths about the dreadful reality of hell.

Place of the condemnation. The term Jesus used to describe this place was *Gehenna*. William Barclay provides some excellent historical background on this word and what it represented in Judaism.[14] *Gehenna* was the Valley of Hinnom, an actual, historical location on the southwest side of the city of Jerusalem (Joshua 15:8). This valley was infamous in Israelite history as the place where Ahaz had introduced the worship of the heathen god Molech in whose molten arms little children were incinerated or caused to *"pass through the fire"* (II Chronicles 28:3; Jeremiah 7:31).

Josiah, the great reforming king, stamped out that form of paganism and turned the Valley of Hinnom into an accursed place (II Kings 23:10). Thereafter, the valley became the garbage dump of Jerusalem where her refuse was cast out and destroyed. It was like a vast public incinerator where there was a constant fire burning to dissipate the odors and consume the rubbish. It was a foul, unclean place where loathsome worms bred on the decaying filth and where the bodies of dead animals and even crucified criminals were discarded.

So *Gehenna* came to stand for all that was accursed and filthy, the place where the useless and the worthless things were discarded and destroyed. That's why it became a synonym for the place of God's final judgment, the eternal Gehenna, the final depository for the moral refuse of the universe—the dreadful place we have come to call hell.

Permanence of the condemnation. Quite plainly, it is described as eternal (II Thessalonians 1:9). That means it is without termination, without intermission, and without alleviation. And there is a moral justification for such intensity. When everlasting creatures offend an infinite Creator in whose image and for whose glory they were created, and then fail to secure His lovingly and sacrificially provided salvation, the consequences are of infinite proportions. It is eternal retribution.

Properties of the condemnation. Finally, it is important to see the properties of the condemnation. Three Biblical phrases, at least, give a vivid insight into the awfulness of hell. The first is *"outer darkness"* (Matthew 25:30). The basic idea is that of permanent exclusion from the presence of God, who is light, and in whom there is no darkness at all (I John 1:5). The picture is one of total isolation and ultimate aloneness. It portrays the depths of self-occupation, which is what gets a person there in the first place. If we provide no place for God in this life, He will provide no place for us in the life to come. It means that me-first in time will lead to me-alone in eternity. The fundamental awfulness of hell, which will transcend every other nuance of penalty which is imposed there, is that God is not there. That means little to the unregenerate man today, but it will mean everything to him in that future day, for only in God's presence and at His right hand can one find *"fullness of joy"* and *"pleasures for evermore"* (Psalm 16:11). Apart from Him, all that is left is eternal woe!

A second Biblical phrase which brings into focus the awfulness of hell is the phrase *"their worm dieth not"* (Mark 9:47,48). Among other things, this is a hideous portrait of the gnawing of conscience and the haunting of remembrance which course through the heart and mind ceaselessly. Doubtless, one of the most agonizing aspects of eternal retribution will be remembering missed opportunities and visualizing what might have been (Luke 16:25).

The third Biblical phrase which relates directly to the concept of *Gehenna* is the phrase *"unquenchable fire"* (Mark 9:47,48). These are terms which describe the horrible forfeiture of eternal life and the grisly thirst of the soul which has been subjected to permanent expulsion from the presence of God into the conflagration, the burning rage, of an eternal Gehenna!

Without doubt, hell is a mournful reality. Jesus spoke of it and warned against it on many occasions. And whenever He did, He did so with a broken heart. And that is how we should speak of it too! Whenever a Christian warns of hell, and only the

most calloused and insensitive would fail to do so, there must be
something like a mist gathering in his eyes. Its undeniable reality
is a powerful motivation for us to do whatever is necessary,
within Biblical parameters, to retrieve lost men, no matter how
ugly their sin or costly our sacrifice.

Are we ready to obey God's commands, love His
creatures and take seriously His warnings regarding hell? If these
motivations will not stir us to do evangelism, what will?

Colonial Perspective

If the first essential ingredient in rekindling the Spirit's
fire is an integration of a Biblical prompting, then the second is
the development of a colonial perspective. People who possess
such a perspective are generally marked by certain distinctive
qualities.

A Wartime Lifestyle

First, there is what has been called a wartime lifestyle.
There's a war going on! Why else would Paul say, *"Put on the
whole armor of God, that ye may be able to stand against the
wiles of the devil"* ? Why else would he say, *"For we wrestle not
against flesh and blood, but against principalities, against
powers, against the rulers of the darkness of this world, against
spiritual wickedness in high places"* (Ephesians 6:11-12)? No
wonder Paul says: *"For the weapons of our warfare are not
carnal, but mighty through God to the pulling down of strong
holds; Casting down imaginations, and every high thing that
exalteth itself against the knowledge of God, and bringing into
captivity every thought to the obedience of Christ"* (II
Corinthians 10:4-5).

It's time for fundamentalists to get past luxuriant,
peacetime lifestyles. We are engaged in a great struggle for the
souls of men. It's a devastating war and the casualties of that
warfare are strewn upon the moral landscape of contemporary
society. Pockets of brokenness, emptiness, meaninglessness and
hopelessness are everywhere present—shallow lives, hollow

expressions, empty hearts, throw-away marriages, abused children and shattered families.

How do patriots live when their nation is at war? I believe they revert to a style of life that is unencumbered with nonessentials, so that wartime effectiveness can be assured. A wartime lifestyle implies that there is a great and worthy cause for which to spend and be spent (II Corinthians 12:15). Paul, in this Corinthian passage, means that he is joyfully ready to impoverish himself utterly, completely, and sacrificially. He will not hold back any resource which is necessary for victory. He is pulling out all the stops. He is withholding nothing for himself, whether of money, time, energy, love, or life itself. He is giving everything for the cause of Christ, the glory of God, and the redemption of lost humanity.

Like patriots in defense of their country, Christians in the service of their King must recover the art of living simply and contentedly. We must learn again the meaning of Paul's words: *"Godliness with contentment is great gain. For we brought nothing into this world, and it is certain we can carry nothing out. And having food and raiment let us be therewith content"* (I Timothy 6:6-8). Christians who are content with the supply of basic necessities generally have a surplus of resources which can be used for kingdom causes. For many Christians this might require a reduction of their lifestyle to a modest level in order to liberate monies which could be managed for Christian ministry. Why is this so important? Piper tells us:

> Three billion people today are outside Jesus Christ. Two-thirds of them have no viable Christian witness in their culture. If they are to hear—and Christ commands that they hear—then cross-cultural missionaries will have to be sent and paid for. All the wealth needed to send this new army of good news ambassadors is already in the church.

If we, like Paul, are content with the simple
necessities of life, hundreds of millions of dollars
in the church would be released to take the
gospel to the frontiers. The revolution of joy and
freedom it would cause at home would be the
best local witness imaginable. The biblical call is
that you can and ought to be content with life's
simple necessities.[15]

I know these are radical proposals, but there's a war
going on! For most of us contemporary Christians it is difficult
to quote Paul's words about contentment and mean them. Our
taste of the "good life" has given us a sort-of silent, unspoken but
very real contempt for the *"godliness with contentment"* life. It
is difficult for us to buy into voluntary abstinence when we're
living out our lives in the midst of voluptuous extravagance. We
are in danger of selling our spiritual birthright, an inheritance
which is both eternal and wonderful, for a mess of material
pottage which is both temporal and undesirable—it doesn't last
and it doesn't satisfy!

Between two vast eternities, we have our little moment
of time, our little vapor of life. What are we going to do with it?
We must learn not only to parrot Paul's words regarding wartime
austerity as opposed to peacetime luxury, but to practice them
from our hearts, fleshing them out in our personal lives and
corporate ministries. In so doing we lay hold of a wartime
lifestyle like those first century Christians did, and in so doing
we liberate both ourselves and our substance, our plenty and our
person for Christ's cause of global evangelism.

A Resident-Alien Outlook

But if the first distinctive quality of a colonial perspective
is a wartime lifestyle, the second is a resident-alien outlook.
That's what we are! The patriarchs all *"confessed that they were
strangers and pilgrims on the earth"* (Hebrews 11:13). Peter
writes to *"the strangers scattered throughout Pontus, Galatia,*

Cappadocia, Asia, and Bithynia," and later in the same book he beseeches them *"as strangers and pilgrims* [to] *abstain from fleshly lusts, which war against the soul"* (I Peter 1:1; 2:11). And Paul describes God's people as a *politeuma*, a colony of foreigners whose purpose was to secure a conquered country for a conquering king. That's Paul's meaning when he says: *"For our citizenship is in heaven"* (Philippians 3:20). He means that Christians on earth are a colony of heaven planted in Satan's backyard!

All of these are New Testament terms which define and set the limits of the Christian's relationship to the *cosmos*. We are said to be resident-aliens, foreigners, strangers, exiles, temporary sojourners, visitors making a brief stay, or pilgrims who are far from their native homeland. It is difficult for us worldly-wise Christian sophisticates to acknowledge, let alone embrace, such other-worldly Christian simplicity. One could very easily get the impression that a significant majority of us Christians are right at home in the *cosmos*. And that is a betrayal of our identity as strangers, exiles, and aliens! All too often our accent is not that of a foreigner at all, but sounds very much like the world-system around us. Our appetites, aspirations, values, and dreams are little more than echoes of the secular society with which we have become so familiar and of which we have become so fond.

Is it possible that we have forgotten whose we are and whom we serve? Are we, like the secular society around us, suffering from a Christian identity-crisis? We are, after all, temporary residents on planet earth, whose outlook, lifestyle, and heartbeat should reflect in miniature the ethic and the character of the homeland. As such, we should refuse to sink our roots too deeply in a cultural and philosophical soil which stands in opposition to God and His truth.

In the book *God's Colony in Man's World*, George Webber suggests that the Christian church as an outpost of heaven is analogous to a small group of colonials perched precariously on the distant shores of a new world. All such colonies, if they are to survive and achieve their purpose, must fulfill three very practical requirements. First, they have to keep their lines of communication to the homeland open, to receive supplies, instructions, and encouragement. Second, they have to stand together, shoulder to shoulder against their common enemies—disease, hunger, and hostile natives. Third, they have to move outside the colony to subdue the wilderness for their king. As a matter of fact, that is their sole reason for existence.[16]

We Christians here on earth must cultivate similar relationships and fulfill similar responsibilities. We, too, must be *in touch* with the homeland, developing and deepening our relationship with God if we wish for our lives to count in evangelism. Moreover, we must be *in unity* with our brothers and sisters in Christ. There is a tragic lack of the practice of reconciliation within fundamentalist churches and fellowships. Nothing undermines evangelism more than this. All Christian announcements of reconciliation to God have a hollow sound if those making the announcements are suffering a lack of reconciliation among themselves. It is not possible to authentically announce reconciliation to the world while we are simultaneously denying reconciliation in the church. Finally, we must be *in contact* with the lost world. That is our sole purpose for remaining behind—moving out into the secular darkness as Christian light and into the worldly decadence as Christian salt, sharing with the lost the way, with the learned the truth, and with the longing the life, which can only mean sharing with them Jesus Christ (John 14:6). This is what aliens, exiles, and strangers do. Is this what we do? Are we in touch with God, in unity with our brothers and sisters and in contact with a needy world?

It may be that we need a reaffirmation of our identity as true, biblical colonialists. Loyalty to such a perspective will become evident when two very distinctive qualities of life become evident: a commitment to a wartime lifestyle and the development of a resident-alien outlook. In such surroundings evangelism begins once again to flourish!

Failure of Christians to Impact Society

Could Christians bear at least a part of the responsibility for the tragic demoralization which is characteristic of our culture? We have found it easy since the mid-point of this century to point our finger at others and indict them—secularists who are independent from God, those anarchists who are revolting against God. Some of us have become experts at verbally flaying such people. But what about us? How have we Christians contributed to the swift and unmistakable development of decadence in western civilization? Perhaps we can best answer these questions by asking two more.

How does a culture give up the truth?

Cultures lose access to the truth through *apostasy*. Apostasy is active departure from the truth and is grounded in unbelief. This is pagan perversity. It is the secular world-system disowning, dethroning, and debunking God and His truth. Cultures also lose access to the truth through *apathy*. Apathy is passive indifference to the truth and is grounded in unconcern. This is Christian lethargy. Truth falls into disuse because Christians have fallen into disinterest. We have other interests, usually materialistic. Woodrow Kroll indicted Christians thus: "We are christians with a small 'c' and capitalists with a capital 'C'." While apathy among God's people is less obvious than apostasy as a cause for slippage of truth in this culture, it is equally as valid.

Why does God judge a culture?

God judges a culture not simply because of non-Christian apostasy but also, and perhaps supremely, because of Christian apathy. Our emotional response to a question like this is to answer in no uncertain terms that God judges cultures due to their pagan decadence, and that is certainly a factor in the measuring out of divine wrath. But a thoughtful response to a question like this would require that we focus not only on pagan decadence but also Christian indifference.

This was certainly true in the case of Christ's penetrating analysis of the church at Laodicea (Revelation 3:15-16). When dealing with flaming fidelity, chilling apostasy and nauseating apathy (hot . . . cold . . . lukewarm), it is clear that in Christ's hierarchy of values it is not apostasy but apathy which is ranked last. Laodicean lukewarmness was repulsive to Jesus Christ. His words *"spew thee out"* mean quite literally to disgorge or vomit. It is a picture of almost vivid crudeness, expressing in the strongest possible way Christ's repudiation of Laodicean apathy. This intense moral indignation against Christian moral indifference has certainly not lessened in the 20th century. Our lukewarmness is as repulsive as Laodicea's. Lukewarmness describes vividly "the respectable, sentimental, nominal, skin-deep religiosity which is so widespread among us today. Our Christianity is flabby and anaemic. We appear to have taken a lukewarm bath of religion."[17] One almost gets the impression in this passage that Christ prefers apostasy over apathy, though it would be difficult to demonstrate that He approves of either. The reason may be that fidelity and apostasy, despite their human imperfections, and in the case of apostasy, human deviation, are matters of commitment, of the exercise of the will; apathy is always non-committal, safe and self-serving. It seems that Christ reserved His most scathing denunciation for half-hearted Christians whose zeal had been reduced to dead ashes, because in such communities of believers the truth is allowed, imperceptibly but undeniably, to slip away!

We are taught in Genesis 18:23-33 that if there had been only ten righteous people in Sodom, even that wicked culture would have been spared. It simply confirms what we have already said. God judges a culture not primarily because of the immorality of the lost, but because of the apathy of the saved. If our culture is not spared the righteous wrath of God, what does that say about God's people in this culture? Is it possible that the

Christian salt has lost its pungence and the Christian light has lost its brilliance? As one author put it:

> If the house is dark when nightfall comes, don't blame the house (that's what happens when the sun sets). The question to ask is: "Where is the light?" If the meat goes bad and becomes rancid and inedible, don't blame the meat (that's what happens when bacteria are left alone to breed). The question to ask is: "Where is the salt?" Just so, if society deteriorates and standards decline till it becomes like a dark night or stinking fish in Western culture, there is no sense in blaming society, for that is what happens when fallen men and women are left to themselves and human selfishness is unchecked. The question to ask is: "Where is the church? Where are God's people? Why are the salt and light of Jesus Christ not permeating and changing the world around them?"[18]

Of course, Christian salt and light can't change everything but we can change something. Too often it appears that we are changing almost nothing. What are the impurities which have weakened us, causing the salt to lose pungency and the light to lose brilliance? It may be conformity—becoming too much like the world; it may be idolatry—worshipping the gods of this world; it may be hypocrisy—wearing the masks of this world; and it may be apathy—expressing too little care and concern for the world. Together these and other deformities have robbed us of the power which is ours in Christ to radically impact our personal slice of the secular society.

As Francis Schaeffer said, "It has been the weakness and accommodation of the evangelical group on the issues of the day that has been largely responsible for the loss of the Christian ethos which has taken place in . . . our own country over the last

40-60 years."[19] But before we fundamentalists congratulate ourselves too much, we must realize that whereas evangelicalism has grown weak through cultural absorption, Fundamentalism has grown weak through cultural isolation. It seems to me that evangelicals have been sucked into the world system, but we have been hiding out from the world's people. Evangelicals can gather a great audience, but through absorption into the culture many of them have very little message. Conversely, we fundamentalists possess a great message, but through isolation from the culture we have very little audience. Tragically, the effect for both is identical: the culture never gets confronted with the truth. What they need is a healthy dose of divine holiness manifested in Biblical separation. What we need is a healthy dose of divine love manifested in evangelistic penetration. And none of this is a possibility until we arise out of the dead ashes of Christian apathy. Perhaps instead of denouncing the secular world we should start repenting of our own sacred sins. Then perhaps we could intersect and maybe even inhibit the slide toward decadence in our culture, as we rediscover and reinstitute urgent and authentic Biblical evangelism in contemporary

THE COST OF THIS FAILURE

Unholy Love	*Unloving Holiness*
1. Cultural Absorption.	1. Cultural Isolation.
2. Sucked Into The *Cosmos*.	2. Hiding Out From The *Cosmos*.
3. Gain An Audience; Lose The Message	3. Retain The Message; Lose The Audience.
4. Need: Ecclesiastical Separation	4. Need: Evangelistic Penetration.
Result is Same for Both: Secular Culture Never Gets Confronted With the Truth! (cf. Prov. 29:18)	

Fundamentalism. No such recovery will be possible until we are prepared to acknowledge humbly the stifling factors which have suffocated authentic evangelism and to aspire fervently to a rekindling of the Spirit's fire. We should all pray that such a recovery will occur soon.

CHAPTER FOUR

PRACTICING AUTHENTIC PROCLAMATION

*Non-absolutists "heap to themselves teachers."
They multiply them because what they currently
have isn't working. Their self-proclaimed open-
mindedness is directly traceable to their empty-
heartedness. That is why we must be there to fill
that emptiness with the fullness of God's
revelation in Scripture.*

"The year—1957—marked the beginning of the globalization of the information revolution: The Russians launched Sputnik. . . . The real importance of Sputnik is *not* that it began the space age, but that it introduced the era of global satellite communication . . . . Satellites transformed the earth into what Marshall McLuhan called a global village. Instead of turning us outward toward space, the satellite era turned the globe inward upon itself."[1] What this means is that we now live in "The Age of Information." In our 200 plus years as a nation we have gone from being an agricultural to an industrial to an informational society. Naisbitt suggests that our whole economy is now based on a renewable and a self-generating resource—information. Our problem is not one of running out of the resource but of drowning in it.

All of this is good news for preachers because we, too, are in the information business. Our business is both to personify and proclaim the *"unsearchable riches of Christ,"* the Gospel of God's Son, the most incredibly valuable body of information on the face of the globe. And where are these riches, this Gospel, this body of information to be found? Without hesitancy we are bold to answer that they are found in Scripture.

We have seen already that perhaps the greatest contradiction in Fundamentalism has been this dialectic of embracing the highest view of inspiration and at the same moment, at least in some segments of the movement, practicing the lowest level of communication. This does not mean that many of our preachers are not good communicators. It means that, while they may have developed skill in the art of communication, some of them have lost sight of the appropriate content. They simply do not preach the Word. They may read from it, talk all around it and even draw out some moral lessons from it, but they have at the same moment failed to tell us what their passage *meant* to its original recipients and what it *means* to us, the contemporary recipients. In consequence, many congregations are compelled to say, as someone has suggested, "Amen to the preacher, but woe to the text." Such preaching will never have the ring of certainty and authority which the exposition of the Scriptures themselves will have.

To preach expositionally means simply to expose the meaning of the passage. To do this we shall have to discern its place in the canon, its place in the specific book of which it is a part and its place in the chapter where it is found. Then we shall have to probe further in order to discover its historical, cultural and linguistic bearings. In particular we shall have to lift out its key words—verbs, participles, prepositions, nouns, adjectives, and adverbs—and we shall have to parse and probe them so that we understand the images and nuances of meaning which they would have conveyed to their original recipients. It is only then that we will be able to speak with authority when we seek to make those ancient truths relevant to the contemporary world. This process of leading out into the open so that all can see, or bringing into focus so that all can comprehend, is what expository preaching is all about. I have no doubt that this is what Paul was commending when he spoke of those who *"labor in the word and doctrine"* (I Timothy 5:17). Paul's word "labor" *(kopiao)* suggests working to the point of sheer exhaustion, and it implies significant expenditures of energy in order to ready ourselves to proclaim God's Word passionately, clearly, and relevantly. It may be that so few preach expositionally because they are not willing to expend such massive amounts of energy. But those who love

Jesus will also love His flock, and will demonstrate that love by equipping themselves to feed His flock (John 21:15-17; I Peter 5:2).

So it goes without saying: we must have a solidly Biblical philosophy of preaching. For our purposes here I would like to lay out *three fundamental ingredients* which should go into that philosophy.

The Matter of Language - Understanding Its Roots

Language Is Eternal

Language is something which has always existed within the framework of the eternal triune God. When we try to think ourselves back into the dark recesses of eternity past, way back beyond the moment when the time-space-matter continuum was spoken into existence by the Creator-God, to a time when there was absolutely nothing but God, even there we find two very precious gifts existing within the Godhead: language and love. Both of these are gifts which require a receiving and a reciprocating object. You cannot love nothingness and neither can you communicate with it. Because the God of the Bible is Triune, there has always been a receiving and reciprocating object both to express love and to exercise speech. This means that language (as well as love) is inherently and intrinsically a part of the warp and fiber of what has always been for it is a part of the God who has always been. To speak is to enter into an eternal and divine tradition.

Language Is Fundamental

Not only is it native to the nature of the Creator, it is native to the nature of the creature. As the image-bearers of God, we, too, are given the great capacity for speech. In Genesis 1:26,27 we are taught that God *created* man. In Genesis 1:28 we are taught that God *communicated* with man. We are given the distinct impression that at the moment of Adam's creation he was given the capacity for speech. He could instantaneously utter and understand language.

Without doubt, this great capacity is a by-product of the image of God in man. God's image in us includes what is:

- *rational*—the ability to think abstractly and to reason logically and analytically
- *moral*—an intuitive grasp of right and wrong, a deep sense of moral ought
- *spiritual*—an innate knowledge of God, a native hunger for Him and the potential for fellowship with Him
- *verbal*—the built-in capacity for intelligent, complex and even symbolic communication

It is this great gift of speech which distinguishes man from the animals. His ability to formulate and then communicate ideas is unparalleled in nature and is unique in the world of living things. The gulf between the chattering of animals and the complex communication system of mankind is completely unbridgeable by any evolutionary hypothesis. Language as we know it requires a special act of creation. As the image-bearers of our Creator, language is a fundamental part of our anatomy.

Language Is Purposeful
Designed for Social Communication

Language, as God gave it, has at least two great purposes. His secondary purpose is that of social communication. This is a subject which deserves a great deal of attention in a fallen world, but cannot fit within the circumference of this chapter because it does not match with our emphasis. Suffice it to say that all social communication must come under the discipline of three Biblical guidelines: the recognition that our tongue can be a great *liability* (James 3:5,6), will bring us into great *accountability* (Matthew 12:36) and lays upon us a great *responsibility* (Colossians 4:6). When thought out, these are sobering guidelines indeed.

Designed for Theological Communication
     But if social communication is language's secondary purpose, theological communication is its primary purpose. God gave language so that He could speak to us, we could speak to Him, and we could speak to others for Him. In the simplest sense, it seems to me that there are at least five species of theological communication:

- *propositional*—God speaks to mankind directly apart from any intermediary, as with Adam and Eve in the Garden of Eden (Genesis 3:8ff)
- *prophetic*—God speaks to mankind indirectly through the office of gifted men (apostles/prophets) who were superintended by the Holy Spirit (II Peter 1:21)
- *propagational*—Christians speak to mankind for God evangelistically, in the power of the Holy Spirit and out of the principles of the Word of God (I Peter 3:15; Mark 16:15)
- *prayer*—Christians speak to God for others and for themselves subordinately, expressing a concern for God's will, not their own (I Thessalonians 5:17; Matthew 6:9-13)
- *praise*—Christians speak and sing worshipfully to God for His glory out of a heart of sincerity and integrity (Psalm 50:23; 9:1)

It is for such lofty purposes that God originally gave to His image-bearers the great gift of speech.
     It is tragic to see how far human language has slipped from its original high purpose. Profanity, malice, obscenity, and infidelity have come to characterize human speech. That's why David warns us: *"The Lord shall cut off all flattering lips, and*

the tongue that speaketh proud things: Who have said, With our tongue will we prevail; our lips are our own: who is lord over us?" (Psalm 12:3-4). Of course, it is not true that our lips are our own. The great capacity for speech finds its origin in God and belongs to God. It is something which comes out from Him and is to be used for Him, in accordance with His principles and for His glory. Any deviation from that purpose is sooner or later bound to meet up with divine retribution—*"the Lord will cut off"* all who engage in such abuses of the divine purpose!

Language Is Powerful

Language has within it both life-giving and death-inducing powers (Proverbs 18:21). In the Hebrew mind a word was a powerful thing. It was much more than a mere guttural sound. It was not simply air forced out of the lungs over the vocal chords, formed and framed by the shaping of tongue and lips. No, to the Hebrew each individual word had independent existence which actually accomplished things in the sphere of history. The spoken word was fearfully alive, a unit of energy charged with power, like a bullet flying to its target. For that very reason, the spiritually-minded Hebrew was sparing of his words. Hebrew speech had fewer than 10,000 words while Greek speech had over 200,000 words.[2]

This idea of the power of words goes all the way back to the Hebrews' understanding of the dynamic power of God's words (Psalm 33:6 and 9; 107:20; 147:15; Isaiah 55:11). They understood God's word to be like a *hammer* breaking up stony hearts (Jeremiah 23:29); a *fire* consuming rubbish in decadent lives (Jeremiah 23:29); a *lamp* lighting our path in the dark night (Psalm 119:105); a *mirror* revealing to us what we are and what we can become (James 1:22-25); a *seed* erupting in spiritual rebirth (I Peter 1:23); *milk* nourishing those who have entered the family (I Peter 2:2); *honey* sweetening the inevitable hardships of the human experience (Psalm 19:10) and like *gold* enriching immeasurably those who have been poverty stricken due to sin (Psalm 19:10). This reverence for the power of a word proceeding from God inevitably came to be applied to the words which proceed from God's image-bearers. It was customary for them to think of a word as something powerful, dynamic, and alive, something which was fearfully charged with energy because it was originally sourced in God Himself. Such a healthy respect for the dynamism of words in the modern world would go a long way toward rectifying the tragic abuse of language which has become so characteristic of contemporary speech.

The relevance of all of this to the task of the preacher is indisputable. Language is the "stuff" of preaching. The preacher's instrument is speech and his agent is his tongue. If this is so, every preacher must develop a reverence for words and skill in using them. Because language is eternal and fundamental, the preacher enters his task humbly and respectfully. Because language is purposeful and powerful the preacher enters his task carefully and precisely. Every preacher is obliged to be constantly stretching in the development of his communication skills and in his ability to clothe his thoughts and ideas with precise and probing words. In summary:

Words must be *Primary*—As something which is native to the nature of both the Creator and His creatures, words compose a fundamental part of the preacher's arsenal. They are the "stuff" of which his thoughts and concepts are made, and without them he cannot express himself with clarity.

Words must be *Precise*—We cannot be sloppy in the use of language. It is impossible to convey a precise message without the use of precise words. Our view of inspiration is verbal not conceptual and our view of preaching should be similar. Great concepts verbalized imprecisely lose their moral weight.

Words must be *Picturesque*—Preachers should strive to become linguistic artisans so that their words paint the picture and turn on the light. Solomon said, *"A word fitly spoken is like apples of gold in pictures of silver"* (Proverbs 25:11). At the very least his simile suggests artistic beauty, significant value and expert craftsmanship in the use of words.

Words must be *Pursued*—The *"labor in the word"* of which Paul speaks in I Timothy 5:17 accentuates the necessity of exhausting exertion in our study of the Word and in our selection of the right words to express its content.

The Marvel of Scripture - Appreciating Its Riches

It is impossible in so short a space to do justice to the marvel of Scripture, but if any one passage comes close to doing so, it would be II Timothy 3:14-17. Paul was always concerned about theological defection, which he understood to mean any deviation from the sound doctrine contained within Scripture. That was his burden in II Timothy 3. In the first half of this chapter he deals with the perils (3:1) and properties (3:2-9) of apostasy and apostates respectively. In the remainder of the chapter he deals with our protection from apostasy, and in a word that protection comes through our tenacious loyalty to Scripture.

Our world is not unlike Paul's. We still live in an era of theological defection. Liberalism denies the credibility of God's Word as though it is not believable, especially in the areas of the supernatural. Neo-orthodoxy denies the identity of God's Word, as though it is not identifiable, by refusing to restrict it to the Bible and by opening itself up to revelatory existential "zaps" where eternity breaks through into time and God's word becomes yours experientially whether you are reading Scripture, the Sunday News, your favorite menu, or perhaps even the yellow pages! Unfortunately, even some "concessive evangelicals"[3] have begun to deny the reliability of God's Word as though it is not dependable. Their capitulation to redaction criticism and their concessions regarding the historicity of Adam and Eve have called into question the integrity of all of Scripture.[4] When men and movements begin to cough up such gems of theological double-talk as "errant infallibility" and "inspired errors," it is time to return to Scripture and let it speak for itself.

That's why Paul's words in II Timothy 3:14-17 are so vitally important. In the face of this kind of defection and confusion, both ancient and modern, the apostle Paul affirms his undiminished confidence in the absolute infallibility of God's Word—an infallibility which allows for no contingencies and which will tolerate no double-talk. He unfolds for us the marvel of Scripture and calls us to appreciate its riches by carefully delineating four of its most powerful characteristics.

Sacred Character

Paul calls the Bible *"the holy scripture"* (v. 15), or as it would be literally, "the sacred writing" *(ta hiera grammata)*. This same phrase is employed by Josephus and Philo and also by Hellenistic Jews when referring to the Old Testament Scriptures.[5] It means that the Bible is composed of messages directly from God, and on that basis it must be conceived of as sacred in its character.

Doubtless the Bible gives evidence of a literary uniqueness. The evidence of this uniqueness is manifold.[6] I shall list five such evidences:

Harmonious Whole

There is in Scripture a remarkable unity despite an amazing variety. Sixty-six books, forty separate authors, a millennium and a half in composition and yet this book is not a heterogenous collection of unrelated essays, but a harmonious whole all woven together around a central messianic personality, Jesus Christ of Nazareth.

Timeless Issues

God and man, sin and salvation, time and eternity, heaven and hell, creation and redemption—these are only a few of the transcendent issues of life which are dealt with in a balanced and beautiful way in God's Word.

Prophetic Precision

There are ancient predictions in Scripture regarding the mode and place of Christ's birth, the quality and character of Christ's life, and the nature and purpose of Christ's death which have been fulfilled precisely and literally. And we can expect that those which relate to His second coming will be fulfilled in the very same way. These predictions and fulfillments can be understood only in terms of the sacred quality of Scripture. Biblical prophecy, interpreted normally and understood properly, is an awe-inspiring manifestation of the divine imprint.

Universal Appeal

It was A. T. Pierson who in the last century described the Bible as "the greatest traveller in the world. It penetrates to every country, civilized and uncivilized. It is seen in the royal palace and in the humble cottage. It is the friend of emperors and beggars. It is read by the light of the dim candle and amid Arctic snows. It is read in the glare of the equatorial sun. It is read in city and country, amid crowds and in solitude." Its appeal transcends all cultural, social, intellectual and racial barriers because its message reaches down not simply into the human head but supremely into the human heart.

Preserved By God

In spite of the perishable materials upon which it was originally written and in spite of the sophisticated attacks to which it has been constantly and ruthlessly subjected, the Bible remains—frequently challenged but utterly unscathed. No book has stood the test of time quite like this book!

Clearly, the Bible has exerted an influence over individual lives, whole societies and entire civilizations which is unmatched and unparalleled in all of history.

Salvatory Goal

The Scriptures are *"able to make thee wise unto salvation . . ."* (v. 15).

When Paul says Scripture is "able," he means that it is powerful. His word is *dunamis,* and that is the term which describes power which is extraordinary, evident, and efficient. If Aleksandr Solzhenitsyn was right to say that one word of truth outweighs the whole world, think of the moral and spiritual weight of Scripture, for it is the mightiest concentration of truth the world has ever known. No word from God is powerless. God's Word *"liveth and abideth forever"* (I Peter 1:23), which can only mean that it never becomes obsolete. On the contrary, it continues to speak truth to the contemporary world.

This power of God's Word is something which Paul relished and in which he rested. It was one of the reasons he was prepared to say that he was *"not ashamed of the gospel of Christ,"* because the gospel was *"the power* [dunamis] *of God unto salvation"* (Romans 1:16). The Roman world of Paul's day was acquainted with power, but it was a power of external things, of military things. Internally and morally Rome was impotent! In particular, the city of Rome had become a "cesspool of iniquity," Seneca said, and "a filthy sewer into which the dregs of the empire flood," Juvenal could say. It takes "power" to liberate people from such bondage, and it was in the Word of God that such power was to be found.

More precisely, Paul says, Scripture is powerful to provide salvation. Salvation is radical rescue. It is deliverance from destruction both temporal and eternal. There were plenty of competing messages in the ancient world, as there are in the modern world. Paul faced Greek intellectualism (the logic of the philosophers), Roman legalism (the law of the Caesars) and Hebraic Judaism (the light of the Rabbis). But none of these messages could do what the Gospel, the message of God's Word, can do. That word is the vehicle through which God liberates and transforms our lives. Paul was taking to the Roman Empire the one message on earth which is sufficient to radically change lives from the inside out for time and eternity. It is *"the holy scriptures, which are able to make thee wise unto salvation."*

Sterling Origin

Paul goes on to say, *"All Scripture is given by inspiration of God . . ."* (v. 16).

Paul's word *all* suggests comprehensiveness. The Bible in all of its parts (plenary inspiration)—Old and New Testaments, miraculous and mundane, Genesis 1-11, Jonah's miraculous experiences and the Chronicler's genealogies—as well as in every word (verbal inspiration) comes from God. We are not at liberty to pick and choose, to dissect, to set ourselves up as judges and then sit in judgment of which parts of Scripture are authoritative and essential and which parts are not.

Unlike the redaction critics, who believe that the authors of the Gospels were not writers at all but editors and that they were not composing authentic history but editing and arranging a biased theology, every authentic fundamentalist acknowledges the authenticity and integrity of the New Testament documents. It may be true that some of the authors of the Gospels used outside sources, but it was only to write true history and always under the superintendence of the Holy Spirit. We would reject the notion that these "editors" put words in Christ's mouth which He never said and attributed to Him acts which He never performed in order to support their own "theology." And we would resist the in-grown tactic of these committees of critics to dialogue, debate and then democratically decide what words Christ actually uttered and what deeds He actually performed. We accept Paul's plain and unmistakable affirmation—*"All scripture is given by inspiration of God,"* and that can only mean Scripture in all of its parts and in every single word! Or as Paul puts it in another place, *". . . let God be true, but every man a liar"* (Romans 3:4).

If Paul's word *all* suggests comprehensiveness, we can be sure that his words *given by inspiration of God* suggest trustworthiness. Actually these words are the translation of one Greek word, *theopneustos,* which would probably be best translated "God-breathed." If it is true that Scripture's source is in the inner recesses of the divine nature and that it was quite literally "breathed out" by Him, then it is equally true that no document on earth is so trustworthy as this document, for indeed *"the mouth of the Lord has spoken it"* (Isaiah 40:5).

It is Peter who helps us to see how this breathed-out word was written down: *"Holy men of God spake as they were moved* [picked up and borne along] *by the Holy Ghost"* (II Peter 1:21). He means that the omniscient Spirit supernaturally superintended both the reception and the recording of the divine message by the human authors so that they were preserved from mental (errors of the head) and mechanical (errors of the hand) blunders. And it must be emphasized that this divine superintendence is indeed supernatural: it is a miracle. As such it defies logical or empirical analysis and explanation. The combination of the omniscient divine Spirit and a submissive human servant produced a theanthropic book, the Holy Scriptures in the same way as the combination of the omnipotent divine Spirit and a submissive human servant produced a theanthropic Person, the Holy Son of God. The inspired book is infallible; the incarnate Son is impeccable. Both entered the realm of human history in essentially the same way—the miraculous synergism of divine and human elements. To deny the possibility of an infallible book is to call into question the possibility of an impeccable Son. Both the written and incarnate *Logos* owe their flawless entrance into a flawed world through flawed agents to the supernatural superintendence of the Holy Spirit. So of course we are prepared to say that the breathed-out, written-down Word of the living God is absolutely trustworthy.

Serviceable Function

Paul also says that *"all scripture . . . is profitable"* (vv. 16,17). Profitable *(ophelimos)* is the word which means, "proving serviceable to the moral and spiritual needs of man."[7] More precisely, Paul states that Scripture is serviceable or profitable in fulfilling three key functions.

Scripture is profitable for **creed**—*the development of our* **belief system**.

This is what Paul means when he says it is *"for doctrine, for reproof."* God's Word erects truth (doctrine) and beats down falsehood (reproof). Truth is that which conforms to the nature of God and the only place to find it unadulterated is in the Bible. So Scripture communicates truth and challenges error—it is *"profitable for doctrine, for reproof."*

Scripture is profitable for **conduct**—*the development of our* **behavioral patterns**.

That's what Paul means when he says it is *"for correction, for instruction in righteousness."* God's Word is for the benevolent restoration of fallen behavior (correction) and the disciplined education which leads children to right moral living (instruction in righteousness). It is Scripture which lifts up the fallen and sets them upright on their feet and then equips them to chart a straight moral course—it is *"profitable for correction, for instruction in righteousness."*

If we long for doctrinal integrity, an erecting of truth and a refuting of error in our lives, we will need "doctrine and reproof." If we long for moral integrity, a defeating of fallenness and an embracing of righteousness in our lives we will need "correction and instruction in righteousness." And there is only one place to turn for such provisions—God's Word, which alone is "profitable" for such things.

Scripture is profitable for **completion**—*the development of a* **blameless character**.

That's Paul's meaning when he says: *"That the man of God may be perfect, throughly furnished unto all good works"* (v. 17). *Perfect* is the word which means "complete, capable or proficient; able to meet all the demands." This kind of proficiency or sufficiency in life is not native, it is derivative. It is something which is divinely supplied not only through the indwelling Spirit but also through the inspired Word. Paul's word, "throughly furnished" is traceable to the same root and simply carries the emphasis a step further: "equipped, yes fully equipped."[8] And this triumphantly adequate equipping of the Christian is not for selfish purposes. It is an equipping "unto all good works." We are not here primarily to selfishly enjoy life but to selflessly employ it for God and others. The thoughtful integration of Scripture into our hearts and lives will set us aflame to help others and honor God. To be sure, God's Word is serviceable in its function.

It is impossible to exaggerate the riches of God's Word. Its sacred character, salvatory goal, sterling origin, and serviceable function clearly set it apart from all other volumes under the sun.

The Mandate to Preach - Obeying Its Requirements

II Timothy 4 constitutes the last words of the apostle Paul. It seems clear that they were penned shortly before his execution at the hands of Nero. The words of this passage are Paul's final legacy to the church of Jesus Christ. They reflect a mood both of great sobriety and great victory. You will look in vain for a note of bitterness and regret, but you will find an expression of forgiveness (v. 16) and of triumph (v. 8). Nor does Paul give any evidence of a morbid preoccupation with his soon and certain execution. Rather, he is preoccupied with the continuance of the Gospel ministry and the well-being of the young man Timothy. In particular, in verses 1-8 Paul seeks to lay upon Timothy the same burden for the ministry which has characterized him. It's a burden which all authentic preachers of the Gospel should share. It seems to me that Paul is identifying for us in this passage *four great factors* in the fulfillment of the mandate to preach.

Biblical Proclamation—Our Message

In verses 1 and 2 of this great passage, we are confronted with three significant insights which relate to preaching.

The Challenge to Biblical Preaching—"I charge thee" (v. 1)

Timothy was timid and the times were tough. Paul knew that he, like us, would be tempted to quit or at least to mute those elements of God's message to humanity that would be most objectionable and least palatable to sinful men. So in verse 1, Paul calls our attention to the coming of our Lord Jesus Christ. This is an awesome motivation to fulfill our mandate to "preach the word." The eschatological implications of Scripture and the great sociological upheavals which they describe are gripping to say the least. No man can truly comprehend the truth of Scripture relating to Christ's coming and remain static. He will be overwhelmingly compelled to purify his own life (I John 3:3) and to serve Jesus Christ tirelessly and energetically (I Corinthians 15:58). In II Timothy 4:1 we are brought face to face with three great challenges.

A sovereign audience. *". . . before God and the Lord Jesus Christ."* Paul's charge was marked by solemnity and sobriety. For him it was a serious moment. He was leaving, Timothy was remaining, and Christ was coming. Timothy could hardly have missed the gravity of Paul's challenge, especially when he calls God the Father and God the Son to witness it.

A sobering appointment. *". . . who shall judge the quick and the dead."* Someday our work will be tested by Jesus Christ. It means that we must perform our tasks as communicators of God's Word in such a way that we can offer them to Christ without shame. We must never be concerned with either the criticism or the verdicts of men, but only that of Jesus Christ. Too many pastors are held prisoners by their peers. They think first of the opinions of their heroes and only second of the will of Christ. Especially in the preaching of God's Word, we should be prisoners of only one Person—Jesus Christ alone! It is with His will and His approval that we should be consumed, for we shall all give an account of our ministries to Him.

A sure appearance. ". . . at His appearing and kingdom." Accompanying Christ's appearing will be the establishment of Christ's kingdom. It should be the desire of every Christian messenger to gain not only an entrance into that kingdom, but as Peter puts it, an abundant entrance (II Peter 1:11).

The Content of Biblical Preaching—"Preach the word" (v. 2)
Anything less is infinitely too little. There's an infinite gap between human wisdom and God's Word.
Paul had already exposed the four grave flaws of man's wisdom in I Corinthians 1:19-25:

It is *impermanent—"I will destroy the wisdom of the wise, and will bring to nothing the understanding of the prudent"* (1:19).

It is *irrational—"Hath not God made foolish the wisdom of this world"* (1:20).

It is *impotent—"The world by wisdom knew not God"* (1:21).

It is *inferior—"The foolishness of God is wiser than men; and the weakness of God is stronger than men"* (1:25).

The only message worth proclaiming is "the word," and man's wisdom simply will not do as a substitute. Paul makes it very clear that we are not to preach our mind, but God's; not our ideas, but God's; not our words, but God's. The preacher is not to spend his time telling his people what he thinks, but what God has already said. Because we are neither philosophers nor speculators but expositors of God's Word, we are obligated always to mine our messages out of that incredibly rich body of truth.

In the ancient world the term "preacher" *(kerux)* had several key connotations. First, it was a *regal* word. The *kerux* was the herald who with clarity brought the message of the king to the populace. He studied to make it plain. Second, it was a *political* word. The *kerux* was the ambassador who, when two armies were in conflict, brought the request for and the terms of peace. Third, it was a *commercial* word. The *kerux* might be the man whom a merchant would employ to shout his wares and invite people to come and buy.[9]

By his use of *kerux* Paul means to say that the "preacher" is the man who brings and makes clear the message of the King-of-kings to his fellow men. Not only so, he is also the man who brings his fellow men into peace with God by announcing the terms of peace, *viz.*, a personal faith in Christ and His finished work. And finally, he is the man who calls out to his fellow men to accept the rich offer which God is making to them in Christ. Intrinsic to this great word are the qualities of authority and certainty. As messengers of the King, it could be no other way, for what every authentic expositor is really saying is "This is what God says." And that is precisely what the contemporary world needs to hear. Modern man is saying, "Tell me of your certainties, I have doubts enough of my own." Only those who preach the Bible will be able to do so.

The Character of Biblical Preaching

It is a *critical* proclamation. We take "critical" to mean essential, necessary, or indispensable. Certainly that is Paul's meaning when he says that Christian preaching must be *"instant in season, out of season."* Paul's word *instant* demands of us a constant state of readiness, and it carries a sense of eagerness, insistence or urgency. The combination of the high privilege of preaching and the desperate plight of the populace renders impossible a spirit of passivity or apathy in the fulfillment of our task. Somehow we have to get past the idea that expository preaching is an incomprehensible dissection of an inexplicable portion of Scripture. There is nothing "dry and dusty" at all about explaining the meaning of God's Word, and nothing which prohibits a passionate proclamation of the discovered truth. And Paul says, this is a readiness or passion which is to characterize us both "in season and out of season." That is, whether our message is received or rejected; whether it is esteemed or contested; whether it goes forth in times of convenience or conflict, we must be ready to proclaim what men need, even if it is something which they do not want.

It is a *careful* proclamation. Paul defines three different ways, at least, that God's Word can be employed—*"reprove, rebuke, exhort"*—and he expects that we will use it in ways which are suitable to the occasion. This means that we will have to be careful and precise in the approach we take to preaching.

Paul's words are not useless hyperbole and neither are they redundant. They are words which were chosen carefully by the Spirit and each of them carries a nuance of emphasis which makes it to differ from the others. To "reprove" is intellectual, to "rebuke" is moral and to "exhort" is emotional. To reprove means to *release from ignorance* by compiling Biblical reasons and arguments. It was a legal term which carried the connotation of beating down the false arguments and erecting the true ones. To rebuke means to *release from sin* by pointing it out without toning it down, with a view to correction. To exhort means to *release from fear* by encouraging and inspiring the faint-hearted. Do we need to reprove? Then use God's Word for convictive purposes. Do we need to rebuke? Then use God's Word for corrective purposes. Do we need to exhort? Then use God's Word for constructive purposes. Authentic expositors of Scripture are to understand this and to use God's truth relevantly and carefully.

It is a *charitable* proclamation. That is certainly the emphasis of Paul's words, *"with all long-suffering."* Long-suffering *(makrothumia)* demands the absence of a retaliatory spirit, especially in the face of resistance, disappointment, and even deep provocation. Most linguistic scholars believe that long-suffering is a distinctively Christian virtue, for the word never occurs in classical Greek and only rarely in later Greek. To proclaim truth *Christianly* one must do so charitably.

The proclamation of God's Word is not always warmly received. The utterance of truth can evoke both the highest admiration and the deepest animosity from the same audience. When God's messenger is faced with that animosity, it is long-suffering which will keep him from despair and the kind of irritability which destroys the beauty of grace that God has placed within him. *Makrothumia* means that the man of God will not give in to the retaliatory spirit, will not give up when the going gets tough and will not get even, even when he has it in his power to do so.

It is a *cerebral* proclamation—"with all . . . doctrine." The Christian messenger must be marked not only by great patience but also by great teaching. This is true because the Christian message is not only a preachment but a teachment. That is the very meaning of the word "doctrine" (teaching). And these two elements of the expositor's task are not antithetical but supplemental; they do not contradict one another they complement one another. So Paul could say within the circumference of one verse of Scripture: *"Preach the word ... with all . . . teaching."* The failure of many fundamentalists to take seriously this Biblical union of preaching and teaching has prompted the explosion of interest among their people in radio and television personalities who are filling the void created by this tragic absence of Biblical teaching. One of the great tasks of an authentic messenger of God is to teach the great moral and ethical implications of the Christian faith to Christian people. This will require thoughtful activity, but it is an activity which is guided and governed by the Spirit and subject to the Scripture.

Cultural Disintegration—Our Environment

In II Timothy 4:3-4 Paul describes two great liabilities which will come to characterize secular society as we move through this age. And they are not designed to discourage us, but to motivate us. The deeper the darkness the more desperate the need for the light.

Secular Society Renounces Absolutes

Paul makes it clear that pagans *"will not endure sound doctrine."* As Colson and others have pointed out, conviction and absolutes are out, tolerance and openness are in. But this is a tolerance which becomes very intolerant the moment it is challenged by an absolute. To suggest something is right or wrong on the basis of a transcendent moral code, such as the Judeo-Christian Scriptures, is to incur the wrath of these otherwise open-minded and tolerant men. This kind of closed-minded openness and intolerant tolerance is bound to prevail in a world where men "will not endure (put up with, tolerate) sound doctrine"—the absolutes of God's Word!

Why this affinity for the relative and this antipathy for the absolute? In my mind the answer is simple. Absolutes give you the ground for determining right from wrong, the capacity to distinguish good from evil. This is the unthinkable thing to those who have denied the very categories of good and evil as a way of justifying a deviate lifestyle. When you banish absolutes you lose the capacity to define good and evil. When nothing can be pronounced evil, everything becomes permissible. This is why pagans exile absolutes into oblivion. It releases them to do their own thing and gives them the false assurance that they can feel good and not feel guilty.

A more perilous circumstance is unimaginable. We must not make light of it or try to heal it slightly (Jeremiah 6:14). In throwing away the truth, they have thrown away the life-line of the culture. That's why we must speak the truth back into the culture and take very seriously the mandate to preach the Word, for without thoughtful and powerful preaching of that Word the culture will perish (Proverbs 29:18).

Non-absolutists are subject to a curious spiritual pathology. They have itching ears and a lustful heart. They want the kind of teaching which pacifies the conscience without penetrating the heart; something which makes them feel respectable but not uncomfortable. And the plumb line or standard by which they choose their teachers and teachings, their reference point, is self not Scripture. So, of course, *"they heap to themselves teachers,"* they multiply them and are always on the lookout for new ones because what they currently have isn't working. In reality their self-proclaimed "open-mindedness" is directly traceable to their "empty-heartedness." That's why we must be there to fill that emptiness with the fullness of God's revelation in Scripture!

Secular Society Embraces Absurdities

"And they shall turn away their ears from the truth, and shall be turned unto fables" (v. 4) Nature abhors a vacuum and so do we. When men turn their ears from the truth, it's no surprise that they are "turned unto fables." *Ektrepo* (turned) is the word which means, "wrenched out of joint, dislocated." The pain of such theological dislocation is incomprehensible. We have only to look at the disintegration of our own culture to see and feel it.

"Fables" or myths (the Greek word is *muthous*) have sprung up around several significant areas of man's being. We are told, for example, in a widely circulated, deeply loved and vigorously defended fable that humans are nothing more than a highly organized system of molecules; the product of countless biological accidents over aeons of evolutionary history with nothing other than "lady luck" or "chance-plus-time" in superintendence of man's development and destiny. It's a myth! It's a biological fantasy, which devalues humanity by denying its Creator and affirming its link with animals.

There are other fables, too. For example, we have been taught for decades that the way to personal freedom is to cast off all restraint. It's what *Time* magazine's sixtieth anniversary edition called "the idea of our age"—absolute, autonomous freedom; the unfettered pursuit of pleasure, the unbounded liberty of the exercise of the human will. It's a myth! It's a psychological fantasy. Contemporary experience confirms what the apostle Peter affirmed 2,000 years ago: *"While they promise them liberty, they themselves are the servants* [slaves] *of corruption: for of whom a man is overcome, of the same is he brought in bondage"* (II Peter 2:19). It turns out that our wills are more weak than free, and that in our uncharactered and unprincipled pursuit of pleasure and freedom, we actually become slaves to our selfish appetites and our weak wills.

These are the absurdities to which modern man has turned, and the results have been traumatic: the devaluation of life; the enslavement of humanity. They are proclaimed as fashionable by celebrities, but they are senseless. And it is only the thoughtful preaching and teaching of the Scripture that will release people from them. God's Word speaks to these issues and so must we!

Personal Preparation—Our Mastery

In II Timothy 4:5 Paul identifies for us four basic disciplines which are essential to our personal preparation for preaching. Without them we shall never become the masters of sermon craft which are so desperately needed in a world which is marked by wholesale defection from the truth.

Be sober—"watch thou in all things."

In a world drunk with myths, Christian communicators are called to be free of every form of mental and spiritual stupefaction by becoming slaves to God's Word. That's the burden of Paul's word "watch" *(nephein)*. While others may abandon the truth, we must vigorously adhere to it.

Be sacrificial—"endure afflictions."

In a hostile world Christians are tempted to silence those elements of the Gospel most likely to be resented. Paul makes it clear that Satanic fables cannot be overcome by an anemic presentation of the truth. We must be prepared to proclaim the whole message, not just its attractive elements, and then be ready to endure afflictions.

Be salvatory—"do the work of an evangelist."

No Christian communicator should ever lose sight of the desperate plight of lost people. They may believe a lie, but we have the truth, and it is imperative that we be willing to work in order to share it with them.

Be steadfast—"make full proof of thy ministry."

Constant badgering from a hostile world may tempt us to fall short of completing our task. That's why this imperative means literally: "carry your ministry forward to completion." It is only as we finish God-given tasks that we are able to glorify God (John 17:4). So we are not to grow weary in the work.

Historical Demonstration—Our Mentors

All of us should be deeply indebted to our predecessors in Gospel ministry. We must never lose sight of that indebtedness or fail to express our gratefulness. What we have in verses 6-8 of this great passage is a sort of biographical sketch of Paul's own life. In it we are given an overview which includes all three tenses of the time spectrum.

In verse 6 Paul surveys his present situation, and the key word is not *death,* but *release—"the time of my departure is at hand."*

In verse 7 Paul summarizes his past accomplishments, and the key word is not *defeat,* but *victory.* Paul has been a combatant in a battle, a competitor in a race, and a custodian of a treasure, and in each of these arenas, God has blessed him with victory.

In verse 8 Paul sketches his future prospects, and the key word is not *despair,* but *reward.* He anticipates a *"crown of righteousness"* because he loves the appearing of the King of righteousness, our Lord Jesus Christ.

All of this, too, constitutes a stimulus to Timothy and to us to be faithful in preaching. Timothy must have been deeply moved by this testimony of the old warrior, Paul. He could sense what Paul was doing. Paul was visualizing a vacancy in the next generation unless the young man Timothy was prepared to take up the torch. Paul had been faithful in his generation; would Timothy be faithful in his? Will we be in ours? Who are the men in our generation who will embrace these ingredients in order to become the authentic expositors God has called us to be? Within our fundamentalist ranks there must be a revival of the practice of authentic expository proclamation of God's Word.

CHAPTER FIVE

IMPLEMENTING AUTHENTIC SEPARATION

"The slide over two generation of time, from lordship (where Biblical principles were understood and external standards where implemented) to legalism (where Biblical principles were ignored and external standards were exalted) to libertinism (where Biblical principles are forgotten and external standards are despised) has produced a scandalous variety of Christianity."

It is undeniably true that Jesus Christ has called His followers to assume a posture of radical non-conformity to the world system. At the heart of the Sermon on the Mount, the manifesto of Jesus, we find these words: *"Be not ye therefore like unto them"* (Matthew 6:8). That is a clarion call for Christians to be different form the world around them.

To be perfectly honest, most of us do not like this "difference talk." And the reason is clear: moral difference does not make for social acceptance, and social acceptance is the one thing for which a good many contemporary Christians are prepared to sell their souls. The world thrives on conformity, it gags on diversity. It is always attempting to force us into its mold (Romans 12:2). "How dare you be different," the world says to Christians, and far too many of us conform.

But why are Christians to be different? Why has Jesus Christ called His followers to be radical, but Godly, non-conformists? It's not so that we can pour contempt on the world. That's what the punk culture has done. They, too, are radical non-conformists, but of an ungodly variety. They refuse to conform, and for some of the right reasons, but in all the wrong ways. Most of the punk culture is a reaction to the materialism and the conformism of the older generation, often their own parents. But this contemptuous reaction manifested in outrageous hair styles, eccentric wardrobes, and shameless lifestyles is not fitting for Christians. Christians are not to have contempt for the world but compassion for its needy people. And neither are Christians called to be different so that they can call attention to themselves. As a matter of fact, authentic Christians are always seeking to divert attention away from themselves and up to Christ.

Why, then, are we called to be different? I believe the reason is two-fold. First, we are called to this radical difference for the sake of conforming to the image and likeness of Jesus Christ. That is a *theological reason.* It goes without saying that Jesus Christ was morally unique, that He was unequalled and unexcelled in His character and conduct. Christians are to aspire to this kind of spiritual excellence and moral difference. We are to become like Jesus Christ. Second, we are called to this radical difference for the sake of modeling before lost men and women the genuine possibility of change. That is a *practical reason.* Lost people need to know that change is possible. They need to know: "It doesn't always have to be like this. I really can change." Who is it that holds out hope to such people? It is Christians who in their values and life styles are modeling the change, the difference, which only Jesus Christ can make in a life.

I have thought often of the despair which must come to lost people when they look at professing Christians who are no different than they are. They must think to themselves: "I had hoped that Jesus Christ might make some sense out of my life. I have tried everything else, and He was my last hope. But as I look in upon these Christians, I am discovering that they are really no different than I am." It is too often true that the deformities of secular society are surfacing in the community of faith. Sometimes we have the same bad ethics, wrong values and self-centered lifestyles; sometimes we manifest the same judgmental spirits, carping criticisms, power politics, and materialistic appetites. So what do these seekers who are looking for a way out conclude? I am convinced that they are saying, "These Christian people are no different. Therefore, the Christian faith must be impotent." That is the tragic price we Christians pay for our eagerness to conform to the world system.

Clearly, there is a need for a carefully defined, Biblically based and compassionately implemented concept of Christian separation. In this chapter we shall try to identify why men resist separation, restate the concept in the clearest terms possible, and try to rescue separation from some of the eccentricities which have gathered around it.

Resisting Separation

Without doubt, the contemporary Christian attitude toward Christian separation is decidedly cool, if not downright frigid. Why is it that this whole matter has fallen on such hard times?

Functional Reasons
To begin with, Christian separation requires disciplined abstinence from what is "evil" and determined adherence to what is "good." Discipline and determination are rare virtues in the modern Christian community. Discipline requires that we deny ourselves but we would rather indulge ourselves. It requires that we lose ourselves, but we would rather love ourselves. It requires that we crucify ourselves, but we would rather coddle ourselves.

Moreover, Christian separation demands a willingness on the part of God's people to be misunderstood, misrepresented, and even maligned by the world around them because Christian values cut across secular values. This clash between two irreconcilable systems of values is what Scripture would define as persecution. Unfortunately, not many contemporary Christians are willing to endure it.

Further, sometimes our rejection of separation is nothing less than a reaction to personalities—men who have tended to be autocratic without being compassionate. These were men who barked and expected that we should bow only because they said it. It's not difficult to see how thinking and sensitive individuals would react to such demands. But, unfortunately, the reaction of many has become a tragic over reaction.

But we should never betray principle because we gag on some personality who may have abused that principle. To do so is to refuse to behave like the mature men and women God has called us to be and to begin to behave like the emotional little children God has forbidden us to be. And the result has been a disastrous accommodation of Christian convictions and conduct to non-Christian culture. Too often there is no significant behavioral difference evident between Christians and non-Christians. Whenever that difference vanishes, the "salt" loses its pungency and the "light" loses its brilliance.

Foundational Reasons

We are Adam's race, and Adam's race does not like to say no to itself. And right there we have the wrinkle! In our culture in general and in the Christian church in particular, there are very few who are prepared to do so. Since the Fall our race has become existential: "Deny me nothing. Give me everything. And give it to me right now!" Unmarried parents, unfaithful partners, and even undisciplined politicians find it difficult to say no to their amorous adventures. Untold millions remain enslaved to cigarettes, alcohol, drugs, gambling, and high cholesterol, high calorie foods in spite of all that is now known of cancer, heart disease, and emphysema. All of it is evidence of a chronic inability to say no. Employees who embezzle, employers who exploit, students who cheat, and criminals who commit felonies all give graphic confirmation to Harvard sociologist, Dr. David Riesman's claim that "the ethic of the United States is in danger of becoming, 'you're a fool if you obey the rules.'"[1] T h i s stubborn reluctance to say no grows out of a spirit of self-indulgence, which will resort to almost any form of deviate behavior so long as one can avoid the necessity of self-denial. It is an alarming phenomenon permeating almost all contemporary social and spiritual relationships. Why is it that we don't want to say no to ourselves or to the world system? Why is it that we don't want to be disciplined, but prefer the easygoing way of self-indulgence? It seems to me that there are two key Scripture passages which speak to this issue and provide a clear Biblical perspective.

Genesis tells us why we don't want to say no to ourselves (Genesis 2:16-17; 3:1-7). It is significant that human history begins with divine **permission**: *"Of every tree . . . thou mayest freely eat"* (2:16); and only then is there a divine **prohibition**: *"But of the tree of the knowledge of good and evil, thou shalt not eat of it . . ."* (2:17). That sets the tone for all of God's dealings with humanity—"Thou mayest" always precedes "Thou shalt not." It means that Christian separation is first and foremost a *positive* dedication to the Lord Jesus Christ, but it includes a *negative* abstention from whatever is displeasing to Him.

So original man was given a choice. There stood before him a superabundant "yes" (every tree—freely eat) and only a solitary "no" (one tree—don't eat). In order for Adam and his race to remain in God's favor, all that was necessary was an act of obedience to that solitary "no." Such an act would have been proof of his love for God and would have confirmed the man and the race in righteousness. But what did Adam choose? He refused the solitary "no." That was the very crux of the fall: the refusal to say no to what he wanted. And ever since it has been our natural disposition to refuse to say no to what we want, to say no to ourselves. Adam's self-centered infection has spread to the whole race.

But if Genesis tells us why we don't want to say no to ourselves, grace tells us why we should say no (Titus 2:11-12): *"Teaching us that denying ungodliness and worldly lusts, we should live soberly, righteously, and godly in this present world."* I have always been struck by the fact that grace, which is rightly perceived to be a very positive and upbeat concept, starts off the Christian life with an emphatic "what not to do." In fact, Paul's word "deny" *(arneomai)* means quite literally "to say no."[2]

It appears that a whole host of Christians have misread grace. In Jude's words they have *"turned the grace of God into lasciviousness"* (v. 4). These "grace freaks" see grace as the total abolition of the rule of law in all its forms. They wish to be rid of the very category of law! For such people rules, guidelines, standards, and regulations have nothing whatsoever to do with the Christian life. Of course, this is a tragic overstatement of what God intended.

Every Christian on this side of the cross must agree that the Mosaic law, as a temporary expression of the moral law of God, has been done away. The Mosaic law has been abolished, and in our day it has been superseded by the standards of grace revealed in the New Testament documents, the "law of Christ," to which Paul, the apostle of liberty, felt he owed a loyalty: *"being not without law to God, but under the law to Christ"* (I Corinthians 9:21). Paul's phrase "under the law" *(ennomos)* means, "subject to the law; obedient to the law; or subject to the law of Christ."[3] And we are told how this "legal obligation" is to be worked out of Christians in the age of grace, *"That the righteousness [dikaioma—*righteous demands or requirements] *of the law might be fulfilled in us who walk not after the flesh, but after the Spirit"* (Romans 8:4). It is our submission to the Spirit and our sensitivity to His prompting which enable us to live a disciplined and Christ-honoring life. The natural by-product of walking in the Spirit is the fulfillment of the righteous requirements of the moral law of God. That's why Paul says at the end of his listing of those jewels he calls the fruit of the Spirit: "against such there is no law" (Galatians 5:23). Of course not! Righteousness never suffers at the hands of those who are marked by *"love, joy, peace, longsuffering, gentleness, goodness, faith, meekness, temperance."* As a matter of fact, Spirit-induced love is the fulfillment of the two tablets of the Law (Matthew 22:36-40; Romans 13:8-10; James 2:8). And as we all know, this kind of love is a fruit which can only be produced in us, not by us, as we depend upon the divine energy of the sovereign Spirit.

So we are given a powerful insight. Our contempt for law in general, and our penchant for refusing to say no in particular are traceable to our racial roots in Adam. But authentic Christians, who have tasted of God's saving grace and have been taught by God's sanctifying grace, understand that they must be prepared to say "no" to themselves and the world system on the basis of God's principles. This can only mean that in the end they will be committed to a Biblical form of Christian separation, refusing *"ungodliness and worldly lusts"* and purposing to live their lives *"soberly, righteously and godly in this present world."*

Restating Separation

We begin with the foundation of Christian separation. The Biblical teaching of separation is founded squarely upon the character of God, especially, but not exclusively, His holiness.

Holiness in Scripture, whether the Old Testament *qadosh* or the New Testament *hagios,* means essentially, "apartness or distinction from that which is common or profane." To sanctify or make holy means simply to "set apart from common use, to consecrate" for sacred purposes.

According to Dr. Rolland McCune, president of Detroit Baptist Theological Seminary in Allen Park, Michigan, the holiness of God is His "apartness" in two realms. First, there is His holiness of majestic transcendence. This describes the divine separation from all that is created and finite, for the God of the Bible is both uncreated and infinite (Isaiah 6:1-3; 57:15; Psalm 99:1-3). Second, there is His holiness of moral purity. This describes His basic separation, apartness or difference from all that is unclean and sinful. God's holiness, McCune says, is the self-affirmation of His being (God is holy). Thus God has a constitutional reaction against anything which contradicts His holiness or is unlike Himself morally. Therefore, God demands that all people, and especially believers, be like Him in character and conduct (Matthew 5:48; Romans 12:1; Ephesians 1:4; 5:27; I John 2:1).

This seems to be Peter's emphasis when quoting from Leviticus, *"Because it is written, Be ye holy; for I am holy"* (I Peter 1:16). While we can never share in God's majestic transcendence, we can all share in His moral purity. God is "separate"—that's what it means to be "holy"—and we too must be separate, for we are called to be like Him. Thus, McCune is right to conclude, "Biblical separation then, is not a foggy notion concocted by some fundamentalist malcontents . . . . It was not pragmatically devised during the heat of controversy. It is of God's very nature to be separatistic as defined earlier, and the demands of separation made upon His people are first of all endemic with the God who called them to be like Him."

If it is true that Christian apartness is an imitation of divine apartness, that immediately precludes all images of harshness, meanness, brazenness, or rudeness as authentic expressions of separatism. God is guilty of none of these deformities, yet He is the prototype for all true separatists. It means that we are responsible to conform to Christ in all dimensions of His morality and that will include both purity (God is holy) and charity (God is love).

Having laid the foundation, we continue with the definition of Christian separation in three forms.

Personal Separation

I define personal separation as follows: Radical non-conformity to the *cosmos*; resolute conformity to Jesus Christ. Theologically the *cosmos* is that highly organized and carefully arranged system of thought and practice which stands in total opposition to God and His truth and is fed and energized by the devil (Ephesians 2:2,3; II Corinthians 4:4; I John 5:19). The Christian, in terms of his value system and behavioral patterns, is not to conform to the world, but instead he is to be transformed into the likeness of Jesus Christ. Christians are obliged to obey the moral imperatives of Scripture, which are stated in categorical and unmistakable terms. However, there are situations which arise in life which are not specifically addressed in God's Word. In such cases what are Christians to do? What are the regulatory principles revealed in Scripture which will help modern Christians to fulfill their calling as radical, but godly, non-conformists?

Expediency

There is the principle of expediency (I Corinthians 6:12a). It is possible for Christians to reach a dissipation level by using up time and energy on things that don't really matter, things that are not expedient. For that reason Paul prays that we will learn to *"approve things that are excellent"* (Philippians 1:10). In erecting our system of values and priorities, it is vital that we never allow the permissible to become the enemy of the essential.

Enslavement

There is the principle of enslavement (I Corinthians 6:12b). To be *"brought under the power"* of anything is to be controlled or mastered by it. Paul is saying that all forms of personal freedom are to be regulated and curtailed by the principle of self-control. If I may be mastered or enslaved by a certain habit or activity, then I must abstain. Christians are taught that they are to *"delight themselves in the Lord"* (Psalm 37:4). If anything other than God is becoming our chief source of joy, it is time to withdraw from it and avoid it altogether.

Enrichment

There is the principle of enrichment (I Corinthians 10:23b). To "edify" means to build up, benefit, strengthen or establish. If Christians might be impoverished rather than enriched, whether mentally, emotionally, physically, morally, or spiritually, then they must learn to say no.

Exaltation

There is the principle of exaltation (I Corinthians 10:31). Every Christian must realize that God's reputation is at stake in his behavior. Our goal should be the exaltation of the divine name, not the gratification of personal appetites. Every activity and appetite must be subordinate to this major consideration. All too often the wicked are given an occasion to blaspheme the name of God on account of the defective behavior of believers

(II Samuel 12:14; Titus 2:5). Preoccupation with such self-assertive, greedy conduct will not do for authentic Christians. If the name of the Lord might be jeopardized, or His reputation compromised, then Spirit-filled Christians must avoid all such activity.

Endangerment

There is the principle of endangerment (I Corinthians 8:9-13). Here is a section of Scripture dealing with our responsibility of protective care for younger and weaker Christians. Only the most selfish of God's people would live their lives without regard to their obligations to be a moral example to their fellow Christians. Maturing Christians, who take seriously their responsibilities to those who are watching them, studiously avoid anything in their lives which might cause others to stumble and fall spiritually. While we must never feed pharisaical judgmentalism, neither should we grow calloused to the legitimate needs of struggling and immature Christians. Rather, we should lovingly defer to the well-being of others rather than selfishly demand the fulfillment of our personal rights. In so doing we follow the moral example of Jesus Christ Himself (Matthew 17:24-27).

Entanglement

There is the principle of entanglement (I Thessalonians 5:21,22; II Timothy 2:4). Paul makes clear in II Timothy 2:4 that Christians on active duty are to refuse to be overmastered by the seductions of "this life" (*bios*—the realm of purely physical and human pursuits). And, in contrast to the contemporary mood of coming as close to the world system as possible while still maintaining some semblance of Christianity, Paul insists that the authentic Christian is ready to follow the divine mandate in I Thessalonians 5:21-22. *"Prove all things"* means to subject everything in your life to the scrutiny of Scripture with a view to either approving or disapproving it. If it proves to be good, "hold it fast." If it proves to be evil, "hold it off." We are called to manifest a godly contempt for what is evil and a godly commitment to what is good. Yet, how many of us do so?

Equivocation

There is the principle of equivocation (Romans 14:23). To equivocate means to halt between two opinions, to be unsure, to be doubtful or uncertain. When Paul says in this verse that we are to do nothing apart from faith, he means that we are not to operate in life blindly. If we have no standard or conviction growing out of faith to provide clear direction in a matter, the prudent course would be one of abstinence.

So these are the principles which, if consistently and carefully applied, will enable us to practice personal separation. Of course, Scripture does not dictate what we should or should not do in every possible scenario of life. But it does provide a series of great principles which we as priests before God are responsible to implement in all the real-life situations of our daily walk. If we are faithful to do so, then we shall fulfill our mandate of radical non-conformity to the world and resolute conformity to Jesus Christ.

Ecclesiastical Separation

But if the first form of Biblical separation is to be found at a personal level, the second form is to be found at an ecclesiastical level. I define ecclesiastical separation as follows: Radical non-conformity to Babel; resolute conformity to the faith, i.e., the body of truth revealed in Scripture.

What does "Babel" have to do with the matter of separation on an ecclesiastical level? Babel in Genesis 11 represents the formal institution of *"the mystery of iniquity,"* the religion of Satan and Antichrist. Thereafter, throughout all of Scripture, Babylon becomes the code word for satanic religion, whatever form it takes. This would include liberalism, neo-orthodoxy, the Eastern religions, which are being popularized in the avalanche of New Age propaganda which has flooded our culture, all forms of the occult, cultists, false prophets, apostasy, and unbelief in all its forms.

The very word "babel" (Genesis 11:9) comes from a Hebrew verb *(balal)* which means "to pour together or mingle together," with the result that confusion is forth-coming.[4] Theologically, "babel" means the distortion and perversion of truth by mixing or mingling it with error. On a linguistic basis in Genesis 11 it meant the end of unadulterated language. On a theological basis in both the ancient and modern world it means the end of unadulterated truth. The real subtlety of "babel" is that it always has a trace of truth in what it says.

This is why authentic fundamentalists have always felt the necessity to be Biblical separatists. They have never felt the liberty to knowingly pour truth and error together, and the only alternative available to them was to separate the truth from error. That is what we call "ecclesiastical separation."

But we learn from history that the Babylonians called themselves not "Babel" (confusion) but "Bab-ili" (gate of God)—"a flattering reinterpretation of its original meaning."[5] So throughout earth history, "Babylon" in its multiformity is always saying: "We are the gate of God." But Scripture is always saying: "No, you are confusion." It's no surprise, therefore, that authentic Christians have always sought to keep their distance, theologically, from "babel," practicing radical non-conformity to it. II Corinthians 6:14-18 is probably the pivotal passage on the matter of ecclesiastical separation. In it Paul presents three significant insights in support of this form of Biblical separation.

The Requirement

The requirement is unfolded in the form of four commands. It is very difficult to miss his point when you are staring four imperatives in the face. What does he say?

"Be ye not unequally yoked together" (v. 14). Historically the concept of the yoke had both matrimonial and doctrinal overtones. "A mixed marriage or cooperation with one

who had a different doctrine was considered to be 'unequally yoked.'"[6] This kind of mismating with something which is totally diverse is strictly forbidden to God's people.

"Come out from among them" (v. 17). The aorist imperative suggests immediate and decisive withdrawal, and the verb carries the connotation of escape as in John 10:39 where it is used of Jesus' escape out of the hands of the Jerusalem Jews.

"And be ye separate" (v. 17). This is a verb suggesting the setting of a limit, the erecting of a boundary or the drawing of a line beyond which we are not to go.

"And touch not the unclean thing" (v. 17). He means here that we are not to meddle with or take hold of the realm of doctrinal unbelief.

Earlier, Paul had made it clear that "Christian separation did not mean absolute isolation from unbelievers (I Corinthians 5:9-10) . . . . Perhaps some Christians had gone to the other extreme by making few distinctions between themselves and the world."[7] While Paul would never call Christians to a stance of complete physical and social segregation from the world's people, he does call them to a stance of ethical, philosophical, and doctrinal separation from the world system.

The Rationale
     Paul insists upon the distinctiveness of the Christian way (vv. 14-16). Paul begins his rationale with the word "for" *(gar)*, a grammatical device which shows a logical conclusion to the preceding clause. What Paul is going to say logically flows out of the prohibition of an unequal yoke with unbelievers. He asks a series of rhetorical questions, each consisting of an antithesis, which will not allow for any synthesis. An antithesis describes mutually exclusive qualities which cannot be blended without great harm. A synthesis describes a mixing or mingling together.

These five questions when combined, present a formidable obstacle to any potential link between righteousness and unrighteousness, light and darkness, Christ and Satan, belief and unbelief, and the temple of God and idols. The distinctiveness of the Christian way is made clear by Paul's insistence that there can be no agreement between these mutually exclusive theological realms!

Paul's rationale is built further on what we might call the uniqueness of the Christian church—". . . *for ye are the temple of the living God . . ."* (v. 16b). Temple means the inner sanctum where God dwells.[8] In his first letter to the Corinthians, Paul had already warned these believers of the dire consequences of defiling the temple, by which he meant the church body as a whole (I Corinthians 3:16, 17). There is no doubt that an "unequal yoke" with lawlessness, darkness, Satan, unbelief and idolatry would be corruptive and ruinous to the church, so it is no surprise that it is strictly and categorically forbidden.

The Reward

Two great blessings are promised to those who obey. In the first place, we can expect a deepened relationship of divine favor: *"and I will receive you"* (v. 17b). "Receive" is the verb which means literally "to receive into, to receive with favor, to welcome or take in." This is good news for those who have been asked to come out. For their act of obedience they will be welcomed into a deeper, more favorable relationship with their God. While such obedience often proves to be costly in a hostile environment, the smile of God far outweighs the approval of the world.

Secondly, we can expect a heightened relationship of divine fatherliness: *"And will be a Father unto you, and ye shall be my sons and daughters . . ."* (v. 18). Paul doesn't mean that Christians who do not practice this form of separation are not sons and daughters. But he means that the people who really enjoy their relationship to God are those who honor God's holiness and truth by identifying with, defending and fleshing-out those great divine attributes no matter the cost. So the call to radical non-conformity to Babel, and resolute conformity to the faith is no "barren renunciation."[9] On the contrary, obedience to this call introduces us to exciting and new levels of the divine favor and the divine fatherliness. This is a reward indeed!

We must be very careful, however, to make a clear distinction between unbelief and unbelievers. Francis Schaeffer once spoke of his very unique relationship with Bishop James Pike, a leading liberal in the Episcopal Church. He described a couple of occasions in which he was able to make clear statements regarding the Christian position "without one iota of compromise," while at the same moment treating Bishop Pike with the respect which is due all human beings. One of Schaeffer's statements is particularly probing: "I will never forget the last time I saw him . . . . He said one of the saddest things I have ever heard: 'when I turned from being agnostic, I went to Union Theological Seminary, eager for and expecting bread; but when I graduated, all that it left me was a handful of pebbles.'"[10] Men like Bishop Pike are definitely not our kin theologically or spiritually but they are our kind creationally. So we must treat them as the image bearers that they are, while never giving away a speck of our Christian faith to their system of unbelief or apostasy.

Also, I feel the necessity to give at least one example of the tragic consequences of failing to practice ecclesiastical separation in the contemporary world. The February 5, 1990, issue of *Christianity Today* carried a fascinating article entitled: "The Remaking of English Evangelicalism" (pp. 25-36), written by David Neff and George K. Brushaber. In it John Stott is identified as "the dean of Anglican evangelicals." Following the Second World War, Stott's tack was to gather around him "a coterie of 40 under-40 clergy who set out to change the face of the church." And on the surface, it would appear that they had succeeded. In the early 1950's less than 10 percent of those ordained to Anglican ministry were evangelicals. By 1969 the figure was 31 percent and by 1986 it was 51 percent.

Superficially, it would seem that the "stay-in" rather than "come-out" philosophy of Anglican evangelicals such as J. I Packer, Dick Lucas, and John Stott has been vindicated. But a closer look at contemporary English evangelicalism paints another picture altogether.

While it is true that the evangelical party within the Anglican church has grown phenomenally over this period, it is equally true that the essential nature of that evangelicalism has changed phenomenally during the same period. From this same article, we find that Dick Lucas, who along with Stott, was one of the founding fathers of the evangelical push in the Church of England is characterized as saying, ". . .much of the effort seems to have been for nought. Expository preaching, concern for doctrinal orthodoxy, the piety of the mind . . . are being ignored or merely taken for granted as the charismatic movement has revitalized [sic] evangelicalism both in and out of the Church of England."

The article goes on to say that Stott himself expresses a similar concern when he says, "I am now afraid there is a liberal evangelical element. People are really going soft on Scripture." The charismatic flavor of British evangelicalism, which with its "yeasty ferment has leavened nearly every part of the evangelical lump," has radically impacted the influence of the postwar leaders. It is no surprise, therefore, that the authors of the article conclude that "a remarkable success by the classical evangelicals has also been a source of discouragement. There is an ever-increasing percentage of younger evangelicals in the Church of England, but their evangelicalism is less and less like that promoted in the postwar resurgence." So profound is this discouragement that, with respect to preaching, Stott is quoted as saying, "I'm in as much despair as Dick Lucas is. The standards of preaching are abysmal, even among evangelicals who are supposed to believe in the Bible."

It's not only bibliology which is suffering in Anglican evangelicalism. Other doctrines are too, according to Michael Baughen, Stott's successor as rector of All Souls, Langham Place, and president of the Anglican Evangelical Assembly. Neff and Brushaber describe Baughen's concerns as follows: "After learning that in the major charismatic songbooks, only one percent of the hymns contain references to the Cross, he fears that the doctrine of the Atonement is being ignored: 'I'm about to start a "red party"—that's "red" for the Atonement. The church has lost sight of the centrality of the Cross.' Baughen is also worried about a fading awareness of sin. 'For many Christian young people today, the greatest sins are experiments on animals and wearing fur coats, rather than the sins that are particularly given priority in the New Testament—such as sleeping with somebody else,' says the earnest bishop."

So, on further reflection, the picture of Anglican evangelicalism is not nearly as impressive as the statistical data might suggest. One feels compelled to ask, of what value is the term "evangelical," when it is being applied to 51 percent of the ordained clergy within Anglicanism, if it no longer represents historic evangelicalism? What enduring value can possibly come from an "evangelicalism" which has gone soft on the Word, the Cross, and the whole matter of sin? Is an evangelicalism eviscerated of an authentic bibliology, soteriology, and hamartiology capable of radically impacting its world for Christ? Should Christians be preoccupied with their "churchly duty" (to quote Stott) to "stay-in" and attempt to reform an apostate organization, as the Church of England with its Anglo-Catholic and liberal branches has most assuredly become? Or would it be wiser to obey the Biblical mandate to *"come out from among them, and be ye separate,"* while simultaneously setting about to build a dynamic network of New Testament local churches which are grounded squarely upon God's Word and are committed fully to Christ's lordship? What would have happened in England over the past generation, where today only 9 percent of the population attend any church, if John Stott and his "coterie of 40 under-40" representatives of historic evangelicalism would have chosen the latter, rather than the former, option?

To the authentic fundamentalist, the answers to these questions seem obvious. Evangelicals who have forfeited historic evangelicalism are impotent to meet the fundamental needs of their culture. While fundamentalists have been accused by Neff and Brushaber of "cultural and intellectual isolation," the kind of evangelicalism which is described in their article is guilty of cultural and intellectual absorption. And absorption into the culture is at least as dangerous as isolation from it, and perhaps more so. What is needed is ecclesiastical separation from apostasy, so that we still have a message worth proclaiming, combined with evangelistic penetration into society, so that we have somebody to whom the message may be proclaimed. In such separation we overcome absorption, and in such penetration we overcome isolation.

Familial Separation

The third form of separation, familial separation, is the unfortunate necessity of functional severance from members of the family who are true Christians, when doctrinal or ethical compromise creeps into their lives or ministries. While recognizing the foundational oneness of spirit which exists between true Christians, we must be willing with sorrow to turn away from entrenched deviation. As with biological siblings, who have become black sheep, we must feel a sense of pain and great loss whenever this necessity arises. This kind of separation is a sort of death—a wrenching apart of what was intended to be permanently joined together. And our heartbeat should be that those who have gone out from the family circle through some form of deviate behavior or belief might return to the center of that circle so that they might be used of God more effectively.

Of course, we must develop a hierarchy of priorities when it comes to familial separation. Over matters of preference we may certainly differ, but we should not divide. We shall have to determine whether or not our dispute is constitutional or merely superficial. If there is no clear-cut *"Thus saith the Lord,"* we shouldn't judge and neither should we separate (Romans

14:10-13). There are two opposite and equally destructive options open to us as Christians. One is to see no basis for separation at all. The other is to see every little difference as a basis for separation among God's people. If the first option is a manifestation of naivete, the second is a manifestation of heresy, which at its root means "a person who without justification creates division."[11] And neither naivete nor heresy will do for authentic Christians.

Moreover, we will be wise to discern whether or not our brother's deviation is an isolated event or a continual pattern. All of us, I think would prefer to be judged by the ebb and flow of our lives and ministries rather than by the eddies, which seem at times to move against the main current. Is our brother's practice or position something permanent or transient? Does it represent a major shift in direction or simply a fleeting moment of experimentation? Is it an appeal for a new and unbiblical theology, or merely an attempt at discovering a new and functional methodology, which might on the surface appear unconventional but is not necessarily unbiblical? The answers to these questions must govern the approach we will take. If the purity of the bride of Christ is not at stake, then we shall have to discipline ourselves against judgmental or pharisaical attitudes and actions toward our brothers with whom we disagree. On the other hand, if a specific behavioral pattern or belief system has the potential to defile the bride, then we shall have to love our brother enough to confront him Biblically, work with him patiently and pray for him faithfully so that Christ's cause does not suffer loss before the watching world. If such an approach is resisted or brushed aside as an unwarranted intrusion, and aberrant patterns become entrenched, it may very well mean a functional severance from our brother as a way of capturing his attention and redirecting his focus to the Biblical issues at stake.

While there are numerous passages in the New Testament documents which touch on the matter of familial separation, it is probably safe to say that II Thessalonians 3 is the key passage. In particular, verses 6, 14, and 15 deal specifically with this subject: *"Now we command you, brethren, in the name of the Lord Jesus Christ, that ye withdraw yourselves from every brother that walketh disorderly, and not after the tradition which you received of us . . . And if any man obey not our word by this epistle, note that man, and have no company with him, that he may be ashamed. Yet count him not as an enemy, but admonish him as a brother."* It seems to me that several significant qualities of familial separation are unfolded in this passage.

First, it is official in its origin—*"Now we command you, brethren, in the name of our Lord Jesus Christ"* (v. 6). These are words which suggest both dignity and gravity. "Command" is the word which was used of "a general ordering his troops"; and a command which is given "in the name of the Lord Jesus Christ" makes it "as authoritative as it can possibly be."[12] It means that we are not at liberty either to actively dismiss or passively ignore this apostolic mandate. We have no more freedom to reject this imperative than we do any of the others which come from the Spirit via the apostles.

Second, it is fraternal in its focus—*"withdraw yourselves from every brother . . . admonish him as a brother"* (vv. 6 and 15). There can be no doubt that familial separation is in view, for we are in this passage dealing with *adelphoi* or "brethren," those who are "born of the same womb." It is within the context of the family that this instruction is to be carried out. Clearly, we are meant to deal differently with our brethren than we do with apostates. In my mind, this is why a distinct category of "familial separation" is so necessary. If we lump our brothers together with apostates under the general heading of "ecclesiastical separation," it isn't long before we are speaking of and treating our brothers as though they were apostates. This is never God's intention, and it undermines our claim to be authentic Christians (John 13:34,35). So while the context is authoritative *("Now we command you. . .),* it is also affectionate *("brethren . . . a brother").*

Third, familial separation is disgraceful in its flavor—*"withdraw . . . note . . . have no company with him . . .*

that he may be ashamed" (vv. 6 and 14). All of these terms suggest the cessation of normal and familiar fellowship. To withdraw means to remain aloof, but not with a spirit of superiority. To note means that the person is to be marked or singled out as one who is insensitive to spiritual instruction. It carries the "flavor of disapproval."[13] To "have no company with" means that in cases where deviation of behavior or belief prevails as a pattern, we are not to "mix ourselves up with" such people. It is a prohibition of intimacy with those who habitually walk (present tense—v. 6) in a disorderly fashion, or with those who habitually refuse obedience (present tense—v. 14) to the apostolic instruction. All of this is so that the shunned believer might be shamed (v. 14). This kind of shaming is designed to humble him, disgrace him, and hopefully alert him to the catastrophic consequences of refusal to pay heed to the Word of God. But his humbling, disgracing, or alerting is not an end in itself, but a means to an end. God "gives grace to the humble" but He "resists the proud." When the man is "humbled," he is in a position to receive grace and be restored. So while the immediate flavor is disgraceful the ultimate objective is beneficial.

Fourth, Paul's instruction in this passage is principial in its emphasis—*"walketh disorderly and not after the tradition... obey not our word by this epistle"* (vv. 6 and 14). "Disorderly" is the word which describes a soldier who refuses to maintain his proper position in the ranks or is out of step. It implies deviation from a set of beliefs or a code of conduct. Paul calls this code *"the tradition,"* which must be taken to mean the authoritative apostolic teaching.[14] In II Thessalonians 2:15 it is called *"the traditions"* (plural) and in 3:14 it is *"our word by this epistle."* Clearly it is to be understood in the broader sense of the whole apostolic theology or prophetic word revealed in Scripture. Or, as Morris puts it, "It stands for all Christian teaching, be it oral or written."[15] What we have here, then, is a broad Biblical principle which transcends the particular isolated event of laziness due to a distortion of Biblical eschatology, which was the problem at that moment in Thessalonica. This means that familial separation is to be invoked in other cases than merely laziness. The passage does not restrict us to such a narrow or limited application. The particular event in this chapter may be indolence in view of Christ's coming, but the general principle is disobedience to the whole of the Christian message as revealed in Scripture. It seems clear from the context that Paul's teaching on this matter in this passage is principial in its emphasis.

Fifth, it is seen to be gentle in its spirit—*"yet count him not as an enemy"* (v. 15). While our insistence upon fidelity to the Word of God must be relentless, it is never to be heartless. Paul insists that there is to be an element of tenderness balancing the element of firmness. There are always those who are overly zealous to point out the faults of others and who seem to relish drastic responses. Paul wants it clearly understood that this kind of action is to be carried out in a spirit of love. "They are to be dealt with; but they remain brethren. Here we have the warm affection of a friend, and not the cold rule of an autocrat."[16]

Finally, familial separation is seen in this passage to be remedial in its goal—*"admonish him as a brother"* (v. 15). While Paul has already forbidden intimate communion with those who are marked by entrenched deviation from Christian truth, he actually encourages *nouthetic* communication with them. *Admonish (noutheteo)* is the Greek word which carries with it the idea of restorative correction. Because it is imperative in mode, it means that we are morally bound to reach out to an erring brother. Because it is plural in number, it means that all Christians are responsible to help in the restorative process. Because it is present in tense, it means that one attempt will not do. We must love our brother enough to repeatedly and patiently reach out to him with the truth. Hendriksen is right to say that, when admonition does not succeed, "segregation must be resorted to."[17]   But this is always the final and most painful step and comes only after repeated and rigorous attempts to humbly, and yet firmly, set our brother straight.

According to Jay Adams, *nouthetic* confrontation consists of at least three basic elements:

1. It always implies a problem to be faced and an obstacle to be overcome
2. It always requires that these problems and obstacles be overcome on the basis of verbal communication
3. It always has as its goal or objective the benefit of the person confronted[18]

To admonish is not to attack, but to assist. Our goal is reclamation, not retribution; and this must be evident as we approach the errant brother.

So these are the qualities which attach themselves to familial separation. The primary application of these qualities is to the fellowship of the local church. But it is difficult to imagine that other authentic assemblies would organizationally affiliate with or support those who have been subjected to the Biblically defined and compassionately implemented discipline of a sister agency. If we are to be authentic Christians, we shall have to manifest the moral courage to implement all three forms of Biblical separation—personal, ecclesiastical, and familial. But there is one final perspective in this concept of separation.

Rescuing Separation

It comes as a surprise to some fundamentalists that separation needs rescuing, but as a matter of fact certain eccentricities have crept into our implementation of this great Biblical principle which make its rescue absolutely essential. While there is room for a great deal of discussion and even debate on this matter, I would like to suggest three simple procedures which might assist us in this rescue operation.

Recognize Its Liabilities
Separation can easily degenerate to the level of the superficial and the external. It is very easy when dealing with this

matter to shift the focus from a Spirit-filled heart where Christ reigns supremely, to a code-keeping mentality where self is applauded regularly. As a matter of fact, I am convinced that this is what has happened over the past couple of generations within Biblical Christianity. Two generations ago there lived a group of Christians who, for the most part, fleshed out their Christian lives under the lordship of Jesus Christ and in the fullness of God's Spirit. The natural by-product of such inward integrity was outward morality, consisting of both dedication to certain practices which were pleasing to Christ and abstention from those things which were not.

Unfortunately, the next generation, the one immediately preceding ours, tended to focus on the externals of outward morality, which had characterized their parents; and seemed to overlook the essentials of inward integrity, which were the real roots of their visible life style. This glaring oversight was further complicated by the fact that their parents tended to pass on the external standards without explaining the Biblical principles. In an authoritarian era, it's not difficult to see how this could happen. The effect was the development of a classical form of legalism (conformity to an outward code as the sign of spirituality), which corrupted true spirituality by shifting the focus from the internal to the external.

Today's generation has in large part forgotten the principle of lordship, which characterized their grandparents and reacted to the practice of legalism which characterized their parents. The result has been the development of a classical form of libertinism, which buys into an unprincipled and standardless form of Christianity, and which is very much like the world, while remaining very much unlike Jesus Christ. This tragic slide, over two generations of time, from lordship (where Biblical principles were understood and external standards were implemented) to legalism (where Biblical principles were ignored and external standards were exalted) to libertinism (where Biblical principles are forgotten and external standards are despised) has produced a scandalous variety of Christianity which is incapable of either confronting the culture or restraining its evil. We shall have to guard ourselves against such degeneration in our lifetime and seek to recover the Spirit-filled, Bible-based, heart focus of our grandparents, if we ever hope to be authentic fundamentalists.

IDENTITY	Classical Libertines (Left-wing)	Classical Legalists (Right-wing)	Christian Lordship (Biblical Balance)
DESCRIBED	Carnal	Pharisaical	Spiritual
EXPRESSED	Throws out rules and principles	Creates and obeys rules with no understanding of principles	Cherishes the principles and understands the rules which are built upon them
ATTITUDE	Anger	Pride	Meekness
FOCUS	Looks at others	Looks at self	Looks at God
SCRIPTURE	Jude 4	Matthew 15:8	Galatians 5:16

Renounce One-dimensional Christianity

I fear that in some circles there has arisen the perception that the issue of separation is the whole pie instead of one piece of the pie. While Christian separation is an indispensable ingredient in the recipe for an authentic Christian life, it is not the single or only ingredient. No recipe for life is really palatable if it consists of only one ingredient. It is the proper blend of a number of ingredients which issues in a well-balanced and savory product.

So we must put separation where it belongs in the Christian experience. No Christian who wishes to be real could

ever abandon this cardinal principle of Christian living, but
neither will he see it as the exclusive principle, which transcends
and makes unnecessary all the others. Those who tend to do this
fall very easily into two destructive traps.

First, they become *inconsistent* in their application of the
whole counsel of God's Word to their separatist friends. What
this means is that a friend might hold to a peculiar set of beliefs,
an eccentric pattern of behavior, or a dubious philosophy of
ministry, and at the very same moment be warmly embraced
because he espouses a form of Biblical separation. And yet it is
these very same elements—beliefs, behavior, ministry—which
become the basis of our alienation from brothers who are not
separatists. This kind of inconsistency has without doubt been
harmful to our claims to be authentic fundamentalists. If the first
destructive trap is inconsistency, the second is *idolatry*. Bob
Jones III said on one occasion that fellowship with God is the
objective of Christ's death (I John 1:1-3), and that prayer,
separation, and other Christian disciplines are the means to the
objective. And then he added this very insightful thought, "If we
substitute the means for the objective, the means become
idolatrous deformities." No one dimension of the Christian
experience should be accorded that kind of elevation.

Recover Attitudinal Integrity

Sometimes we fundamentalists are militant biblicists
when it comes to affirmational propositions in Scripture—our
doctrines. However, when it comes to attitudinal propositions in
Scripture—our demeanor—we are not so militant. We will be truly
Biblical only when we can support with equal vigor a militancy
for the message of Christ and a militancy for the meekness of
Christ. I have often thought that perhaps a good title for a book
dealing with this much needed balance within Fundamentalism
might be *Militant Meekness*.

Scripture is clear regarding the necessity of attitudinal
integrity:

We are called to manifest *"the meekness and gentleness of Christ,"* for though we *"walk in the flesh, we do not war after the flesh: (For the weapons of our warfare are not carnal, but mighty through God to the pulling down of strongholds)"* (II Corinthians 10:1-3).

We are called to *"speak the truth in love"* (Ephesians 4:15). Without doubt, authentic Christians are lovers of the truth, but they have purposed never to speak it brutally or cruelly.

We are called to weeping in the face of tragic compromise: *"Brethren, be followers of me, and mark them which walk so as ye have us for an ensample. (For many walk, of whom I have told you often, and now tell you even weeping, that they are the enemies of the cross of Christ)"* (Philippians 3:17,18).

We are called to be utterly uncontentious in the midst of our contending for the truth: *"And the servant of the Lord must not strive; but be gentle unto all men, apt to teach, patient, in meekness instructing those that oppose themselves; if God peradventure will give them repentance to the acknowledging of the truth; And that they may recover themselves out of the snare of the devil, who are taken captive by him at his will"* (II Timothy 2:24-26).

This attitudinal balance to which we should all aspire, combined with a subtle hint as to how we might achieve it, is expressed very clearly in an excerpt from Peter Kreeft's book, *Making Choices.* Kreeft says:

So in waging spiritual warfare we must avoid both the ancient, "hard" mistake and the modern, "soft" mistake. Our ancestors were better than we are at the "hard" virtues, like courage and chastity. We are better at the "soft" virtues, like kindness and philanthropy. But you can no more specialize in virtue than in anatomical organs. The virtues are like organs in a body; interdependent. Compassion without courage ceases under pressure, and compassion without justice is wasted. Justice without mercy becomes cruelty; chastity without charity, coldness. The "hard" virtues are like the bones in a body, and the "soft" virtues like tissues. Bones without tissues are a skeleton; tissues without bones, a jellyfish.

How can we learn to fight without hating, to hate sins but not sinners, to love sinners without loving sins? Only one ever did it perfectly. The only way we can do it is his way. He *is* "the way, the truth, and the life." If he only *taught* the way, we could learn it from others. But if he is the way, we can learn it and live it only in him.[19]

So these are the procedures which are essential to rescuing separation from the eccentricities which have gathered all around it. We must recognize its liabilities, renounce one-dimensional Christianity and recover attitudinal integrity. In this way we shall be able to reclaim an authentic variety of separation for Fundamentalism.

It is our earnest hope that the next generation of fundamentalists will be deeply committed to a carefully defined, Biblically based and compassionately implemented concept of Christian separation. In manifesting such "radical difference," they become models of conformity to Christ and of change before the lost world. In this way God is honored and humanity is helped.

CHAPTER SIX

RECOVERING OUR SPIRITUAL VITALITY

"To follow the living Christ inevitably and radically alters our opinions, values, and behavioral patterns every day! Christians were never meant to be feeble echoes of the world system, but radical alternatives to it."

Fundamentalism stands in need of revival. The basic solution to the problems which plague us and the potential which evades us is nothing less than a healthy dose of Biblical revival. Only then will we be able to recover our spiritual vitality and realize our role as ambassadors. But what is revival?

It sometimes takes more than a dictionary to define the meaning of a word, especially if the word in question has something to do with human experience. Words which describe an experience have a basic dictionary meaning, but it is real life situations which define the intensity of that meaning. Clearly the word "pain" means something quite different to a person who has always enjoyed good health than to a person who has passed through the furnace of physical agony in a cancer ward.

The same is true of the term revival. To a flag-waving marine sergeant, revival might mean the restoration of America to its rightful place of economic, political, and military leadership in the world community. To such people revival equals "Save America." But what if we lost America like the Chinese lost China and the Polish lost Poland? Could we still have revival? Is it contingent on political structures? There is evidence that the church is much more alive in China and Eastern Europe than it is in America.

To a covetous Christian businessman, all aglow in his navy blue business suit, revival might mean the preservation of our affluent life-styles, the elimination of inflation, recession, or depression, and the protection of our opulent possessions and potent positions. To such people revival equals "Save my economic interests." But what if we lost everything? What if all the props were knocked out from under us, and all we had left was God? Would He be enough? Could we still have revival? Is it contingent on economic structures?

To an aggressive, ambitious, energetic zealot for Christ, revival might mean exploding statistics, bulging budgets, expanding properties, multiplying staff, and monumental facilities. To such people revival equals "Save my reputation for 'success.'" But what if our church is in some remote corner of rural America or some obscure village or secular city on the foreign mission field? Could we still have revival? Is it contingent on extravagant and exploding surroundings?

Revival can mean different things to different people. But what does it mean to God? Perhaps the greatest text in Scripture on the subject of revival is II Chronicles 7:14. As Walter Kaiser has demonstrated, its centrality can be seen in the fact that it provides the outline for II Chronicles and sets the agenda for the description of five key Davidic kings of Judah. "Each of the four conditions for revival is taken up separately as the single most important term for the reigns and lives of these five Judean monarchs."[1]

"Humble Yourselves"	Describes Rehoboam	II Chron. 11-12
"Seek My Face"	Describes Asa	II Chron. 14-16
"Pray"	Describes Jehoshaphat	II Chron. 17-20
"Turn from your wicked ways"	Describes Hezekiah	II Chron. 24-32
"Humble Yourselves"	Describes Josiah	II Chron. 34-35

It may be that the condition of humility is employed a second time, forming what Kaiser calls an inclusio (the first and last king sharing the same term), because it is so fundamental to revival.

In the simplest sense, revival is "the restoration of something to its true nature and purpose."[2] It is the visible evidence of a dynamic God-life within a community of believers. II Chronicles 7:14 lays out for us four essential ingredients which reveal the nature of revival.

The Constituents of Revival

Revival is for all those who are owned by God and have His name upon them, *"If my people, which are called by my name."* What God names He owns, and what God owns He both protects and rules. If we are not subject to His rule, we might question whether we should be called by His name. It's a simple equation. Those who are not God's people have no need of God's revival, for revival implies restoration of life; and those who are not God's people have no life from God at all. Their need is not for restoration, but for regeneration.

There is no doubt that God's people at the end of the twentieth century in the Western world have a desperate need for revival. We are a people addicted to comfort, convenience, and cash; obsessed with position, prestige, and power; encrusted with traditionalism and infected with materialism, hedonism, and me-ism. These are the gods to which not only modern man but Christian men bow down.

Charles Colson observed that we're not unlike Ray Kroc, the founder of McDonalds, who when he was asked by the *New York Times* what he believed in responded by saying, "God, my family, and McDonald's hamburgers." But then he added, "And when I get to the office I reverse the order." There's a certain irony in that facetious comment. For many Christians, God has first priority on Sunday mornings, but life goes on as usual the rest of the week. We kind of privatize our Christian experience and pigeon hole it for one day a week. It gives us a good inward feeling on Sunday, but we would never allow it to affect our outward actions on Monday, Tuesday, or Wednesday!

But being a Christian is much more than mouthing pious hymns, parroting our favorite verses, and believing in some distant, remote, invisible, and irrelevant deity one day a week! To follow the living Christ inevitably and radically alters our opinions, values, and behavioral patterns every day! Christians were never meant to be feeble echoes of the world system but radical alternatives to it.

This total and radical alteration is conspicuous by its absence in so many of our lives. "Echoes" are "more of the same." And too often that's all you see when you look at the church standing alongside the world—more of the same!

The Concern of Revival

At the heart of revival is a passionate preoccupation with God's name: *"My people, which are called by my name."* The concern of revival is not saving my country, my bank account or my church. Human prosperity does not enter the picture at all, only God's glory! But it is only a revived people who will aspire to and live energetically for the exaltation of His name.

But is this really how we live? Isn't it too often true that we are infected with idolatry, betraying the God whose name is One; with apathy, betraying the God whose name is Love; with hypocrisy, betraying the God whose name is True; and with impurity, betraying the God whose name is Holy. God's great name means far too little to us who are so selfishly preoccupied with our own puny name.

That's why the concern of revival, it's central burden and most impassioned obsession is the restoration of God's name to the exalted position which it deserves in our lives and culture. In revival there is no room for self-centered motivation, only hunger for divine exaltation!

The Conditions of Revival

Brokenness

"*If my people . . . shall humble themselves.*" This is the fount of all the rest. The Hebrew for humble means at its root, "to bend the knee," the visible symbol of an inward submission. It means to be subdued, brought low, under, or into subjection. In a word, it describes surrender or brokenness.

To whom are we to surrender or manifest such brokenness? Of course, it is to God Himself. We are to be broken before Him! I find myself agreeing with P. Carnegie Simpson's portrayal of Jesus Christ in a book he wrote in 1930 entitled, *The Fact of Christ*:

> Jesus is not one of the group of the world's great. Talk about Alexander the Great and Charles the Great and Napoleon the Great if you will . . . Jesus is apart. He is not the Great; he is the Only. He is simply Jesus. Nothing could add to that . . . He is beyond our analysis. He compels our criticism to overleap itself. He awes our spirits. There is a saying of Charles Lamb . . . that "if Shakespeare was to come into this room, we should all rise up to meet him, but if that Person was to come into it, we should all fall down and try to kiss the hem of his garment."

That is where we all belong whenever we are in the presence of Jesus Christ—on our faces before Him, expressing our complete submission as His redeemed children and His humble servants.

But what does it mean to be broken? What is it that we are to surrender to our great God? It is our self-sovereignty, the strength of our will, our prideful pursuit of power and position. Brokenness means that we must reduce to rubble our hunger for self-preservation and self-exaltation, our preoccupation with what others think, our intensity when it comes to my will and our apathy when it comes to God's will. Brokenness demands the shattering of the human will for the sake of serving the divine will. It requires that we abandon the tendency to please and fear men so that we become God-fearers not man-fearers and God-pleasers not man-pleasers! All of this and more is what it means to be broken before God.

What is needed is a humble recognition of our own self-centered pride, combined with a repudiation of our native propensity to be power seekers rather than servant leaders. In a word, what we need is radical revival: spiritual renewal in the very heart and core of our being.

But this can never come without brokenness, without prostrating ourselves before God, without admitting our contemptuous forms of pride, without acknowledging our Adam-like hunger for God-like power, without recognizing our utter weakness and absolute helplessness apart from God and without renouncing our self-sovereignty by crucifying our self-centeredness. It's then that we learn that in human weakness we enjoy divine strength and that it is in our position in Christ not our prominence in the world that we find meaning and power.

For us it is no longer "the will to power" as Nietzsche said, but "the will to surrender" as Jesus said. *"If my people. . . shall humble themselves"*—that is the first and most important condition. When this takes place all the rest will naturally follow.

Prayerfulness

Once we are broken we have no alternative. Broken people are completely dependent upon God, and prayer is the supreme vehicle by which that dependence is made evident. They are no longer finding their resources within themselves but in God.

What is prayer? Prayer is an acknowledgment of humanity's limited perception. It is the brightest man saying to God "I have no wisdom; I am ignorant." So we bring our ignorance up into the presence of God's omniscience and draw upon it. Prayer is also an acknowledgment of humanity's limited power. It is the strongest man saying to God, "I have no strength; I am impotent." So we bring our impotence up into the presence of God's omnipotence and draw upon it. That is prayer, and the praying which is effective always carries with it a sense of desperation and deep need.

Jehoshaphat, king of Judah, is an example of one who was prepared to acknowledge his utter dependence upon God. In II Chronicles 10:12, we see him crying out to God in prayer in the face of an imminent invasion by the Ammonites, Moabites, and Edomites—three of Israel's most implacable enemies. One can almost hear the ring of desperation in his words as he prays, *"O our God, wilt thou not judge them? For we have no might against this great company* [here is a strong man admitting his impotence] . . . *neither know we what to do:* [here is a bright man admitting his ignorance] *but our eyes are upon thee"* [here is a surrendered man—a broken man—looking to God's omnipotence and omniscience].

Prayer is not only an act of desperation, but it is also an act of discipline. In fact, Jesus taught in Matthew 6:5-8 that there are at least five disciplines attached to the issue of prayer.

Prayer—a Discipline of Time

"When thou prayest" (6:5). Jesus does not say, "if," He says "when." That can only mean that He assumes we will pray and that prayer is an intrinsic part of what Christians do. "When" is a temporal particle suggesting the concept of time. We have time for whatever is important to us, whatever fits into our hierarchy of values and our schedule of priorities. All Christians are called to *"redeem the time"* (Ephesians 5:16), that is, to release it from its evil bondage by using it for divine purposes. One of the most profound ways in which we do that is by faithfully engaging in the discipline of prayer.

Prayer—a Discipline in Humility

"*Enter into thy closet*" (6:6). This stands in stark contrast
to the hypocrites who loved to pray "*standing in the synagogues
and in the corners of the streets, that they may be seen of men*"
(6:5). The Jewish system of prayer made ostentation very easy.
The Jew prayed standing with his hands outstretched, palms
upward, and his head bowed. Prayer had to be said at 9 a.m., 12
noon, and 3 p.m., and it had to be said wherever a man might be
at those hours.[3] It was not difficult for a man to make sure that
at these times he was at a busy street corner, in a crowded city
square or perhaps on the top step of the entrance to the
synagogue so that all might admire his piety. But we can be sure
that whenever we pray so that men might see, God will neither
hear nor bless.

Interestingly, Matthew's word for closet is *tameion*. It is
a word which was used for the storeroom where treasures were
often kept.[4] There are great treasures in the secret presence of
God.

Prayer—a Discipline of the Mind

"*Shut thy door*" (6:6). Genuine prayer requires undivided
attention. We are to love the Lord our God with all our heart,
soul, strength, and mind! God will have none of our half-
heartedness. Especially in the discipline of prayer there must be
a wholehearted concentration and devotion, and this will
inevitably mean the elimination of all possible distractions—"shut
thy door."

Prayer—a Discipline of Intimacy

"*Pray to thy Father*" (6:6). Authentic prayer is based on
our union with God through Christ. That which gives real
efficacy to our prayers is the fact that they are wrapped all
around with the finished work of Christ on Calvary, and on that
basis they ascend into the throne room as a "*sweet-smelling
savor*" (Ephesians 5:2). Christians are the only people on earth
who can call God their "Father" and be free of hypocrisy for they

have been born again into God's family. And with that new birth
has come the sensitive heart, the listening ear, and the powerful
hand of God, all of which are moved into operation in
humanity's behalf by the prayers of God's children.

Prayer—a Discipline of Communication
    "Use not vain repetitions" (6:7). To repeat a request is
quite proper, but to parrot words that are not expressions of our
heart, so as to gain indulgences or to accumulate merit is
impotent. God is interested in reality not ritual, in spiritually
induced prayer not mechanically induced prayer and in that
which springs supremely from devotion not merely from duty.
    How do Christians learn to talk with God in prayer? We
learn to express ourselves in prayer by acquainting ourselves with
God's thoughts revealed in Scripture. This is especially true as
we study the great prayers recorded in God's Word. As you learn
to think God's thoughts after Him, you learn to talk with God as
you kneel before Him. It is by developing this capacity that we
learn to express ourselves in true prayer. Our petitions must
always ascend to the throne-room not out of an empty mind (vain
repetitions), but out of a full heart—one which is saturated with
Scripture.
    Do we want to experience revival on a national level?
Then this kind of transparent prayerfulness will have to follow
our total brokenness. How tragically delinquent so many of us
have been in this matter of prayer.

Wholeheartedness
    *"If my people . . . shall humble themselves, and pray,
and seek my face . . ."* Sin makes us fugitives from the face of
God. Adam and his wife knew this only too well, for the
Scripture says that after their transgression in the garden they
"hid themselves from the presence of the Lord . . . " (Genesis
3:8). Interestingly, the Hebrew word for "presence" is "face."
Literally, we are being told that Adam and Eve hid themselves
from "the faces of God." Their customary meeting with the Lord

in "the cool of the day" had been transformed due to sin. Always before they had looked forward to it with a sense of joyful anticipation, but on this day they faced it with a sense of fearful apprehension. These daily appearances of God had been their opportunities to see the eternal God brought into focus. But on account of their sin they could no longer look up into His face without a sense of fear, shame, and guilt. Sin had defiled the pristine warmth and love of the divine-human relationship, and that defilement will be with unregenerate humanity until the end of the ages (Revelation 6:16; 22:3,4).

Notwithstanding, in spite of our original parents' sin, God took the initial step in approaching the fallen couple. It was symbolic of His intentions for all of humanity. This initial approach was only the first step in a long series of steps that would lead the eternal Son of God to a Jewish womb, a Bethlehem manger, a Nazareth carpenter's bench and ultimately a Roman cross in order to achieve our salvation. Because that is so, it is now possible for us to once again seek God's face.

To "seek God's face" means to "hunger and thirst" after His presence and power in our lives. Moses' use of this imagery in Deuteronomy 4:29 means that "God binds His people to love and serve Him as the first principle of their living."[5]

Not many of us have known the gnawing emptiness of real hunger, nor the parched agony of real thirst. But to those who daily faced the harsh realities of drought and desert in a Palestinian wasteland,these words meant something. Theirs was "no genteel hunger which could be satisfied with a mid-morning snack," nor was it a simple thirst which could be "slaked with a cup of coffee or an iced tea."[6] No, to seek God's face pictures the hunger of the man who is emaciated and perishing for lack of food, and the thirst of the man whose tongue is parched and splitting due to its dehydration, and who will die unless he drinks of the life restoring water.

So the question is "How much do you want revival?" How greatly do you long for a demonstration of what only God can do in your personal life, your family unit, your spiritual ministry, and your entire culture? Is there a yearning for manifestations of a divine working which cannot be explained away in purely human terms? Do we hunger and thirst for a Biblical revival as much as a starving man craves for food and a dying man lusts for water? If so, it means that we will seek God's face, both in Scripture and in prayer, with the same intensity and wholeheartedness as though our very lives depended upon it. For it is only when we search for Him with all our heart that we are promised we shall find Him (Jeremiah 29:13). The broken and prayerful heart must now approach God with the whole heart.

Decisiveness

"If my people . . . shall humble themselves, and pray, and seek my face, and turn from their wicked ways . . ." Brokenness, prayerfulness, and wholeheartedness cannot survive, cannot even commence, in the midst of sinfulness. One cannot seek God's face until he is prepared to turn from his sin whatever form it may take.

To turn from our wicked ways means repudiation of all known sin combined with an affirmation of God's total will for our lives. It means no longer *"counting our lives dear unto ourselves"* (Acts 20:24; Matthew 10:39), no longer building an ethic for our pride, no longer covering up as though nothing was wrong and everything was fine. It means embracing objectivity, integrity, and transparency in dealing with our apathy and artificiality. It means "ultimate honesty"—uncovering everything, justifying nothing, imputing blame to no one, and making a decisive break with it all, slaying the dragons of pride and self-righteousness.

So we are taught clearly that revival is not simply a warm, tingling feeling, like a Mormon conversion, but a decisive decision of an enlightened and convicted will in which I cease justifying sin and start living in the power of the Holy Spirit and on the basis of the Holy Scriptures because I really am a justified sinner. Revival is not simply an ecstatic emotion, it is supremely an emphatic volition!

This takes the phenomenon of revival out of the sphere of the superficial and places it in the sphere of the substantial. Its focus is not simply happiness, but holiness. Because this is so, revival can never be cheap. It is a costly thing to break with our wicked ways. It will cost us our sin and our self, and both sin and self are powerful spiritual principles which relinquish their hold on their victims very reluctantly and with great difficulty. Still, if we aspire to Biblical revival, we shall have to be ready to pay even this price by turning from our wicked ways.

The Consequence of Revival

We Gain God's Listening Ear
"Then will I hear from heaven." I fear that like Israel in her spiritually diseased state, God is saying to His corrupted and crippled Church, *"Yea, when ye make many prayers, I will not hear: your hands are full of blood"* (Isaiah 1:15). Hands "full of blood" certainly represent a morality which is foreign to brokenness, prayerfulness, wholeheartedness, and decisiveness. So long as a body of believers harbors and justifies sin, God will not hear, heaven will not open and revival will not fall.

But just the opposite is equally true. God's ear is tuned to the cry of His children who are prepared from their hearts to satisfy the conditions for revival. And there is power in that listening ear for it arouses into action in the behalf of His people God's mighty arm and His powerful right hand.

We Gain God's Forgiving Heart
"And will forgive their sin." Unforgiven sin is the most serious condition in the human experience. For the unbeliever it means hell, the horrible reality of permanent and irrevocable

banishment from the presence of God in *Gehenna*. For the believer it means barrenness and uselessness on earth as well as shame and loss at the *Bema*.

The real tragedy of Christian sin lies in the fact that the culture in which they live is left unchallenged. And whenever a culture is left to itself, it deteriorates and ultimately disintegrates as it falls under the judgment of God. But every Christian must remember that God does not judge a culture primarily because of non-Christian immorality, but supremely because of Christian apathy and artificiality. While we Christians seem to find it very easy to castigate secular society, if we were perfectly honest, perhaps we would have to castigate ourselves first. It may be that our culture is infected with moral decadence because so many of us Christians are infected with moral indifference. This was certainly true in Sodom and Gomorrah. God's hand of judgment against those immoral cities would have been stayed, if only ten authentic believers could have been found (Genesis 18:23-33). But, alas, they were not there.

So it is imperative that we Christians keep short accounts with God and be sure that we daily capitalize upon His Fatherly forgiveness. This will mean that we shall have to turn repentantly from all that we know to be displeasing to His holy love, claim humbly the cleansing power of Christ's atoning blood and open believingly every particle of our anatomy to His searching scrutiny and sovereign control. Then, when we have met the conditions for revival, not only will God's ear be open to us, but so will His heart. This will mean that He both hears our confession and forgives our sin. It is then that the forgiven people of God can once again begin to impact their culture as pungent salt and brilliant light.

We Gain God's Healing Hand

"And will heal their land." In the Old Testament theocracy this meant that Israel could expect political ascendancy and material prosperity, but in the New Testament church it

means that Christ's bride can expect moral vitality and spiritual potency. The wounds inflicted on our culture as a result of Christian apathy and non-Christian immorality can only be remedied or cured through the impact of a revived church.

Isn't it true that moral and spiritual prosperity are really what we need? We already have material abundance, everything we could possibly want. What we don't have is everything that we so desperately need. It seems to me that we have developed in this culture a generation of believers, and this is true of us who fit within the fundamentalist mainstream too, who have become extremely efficient at providing for our families and ourselves what we want, and extremely inept at providing what we need. What we want is material, what we need is spiritual. We need the presence and the power of God in revival. When that happens not only will Christians be rejuvenated spiritually, the culture will be impacted morally. God will "heal their land."

Those of us within the fundamentalist orbit, who aspire to see revival in Christ's church and in American culture, will have to deal honestly with some probing questions.

How concerned are we for God's name? How often does a preoccupation with our name get in the way of the exaltation of God's name?

Are we a broken people, prostrating ourselves before Him and surrendering to Him, or have we fallen prey to the "will to power?" Are we touchy about our position or title and anxious to catch the public eye? We may as well call it what it is: sin and self-centered pride! Those who think themselves to be something will do nothing that lasts. Those who are learning to be nothing will surely do something for God which endures.

The discipline of prayer, the hunger for God's face, the break with sin (pray, seek, turn)—are these the patterns which characterize our lives, the burdens which we carry in our hearts?

Our answers to these questions will tell us whether or not we shall ever become the authentic fundamentalists which our culture so desperately needs.

FOOTNOTES

Preface
[1]*U.S. News & World Report*, February 22, 1993. p. 52.

Chapter 1
[1]Quoted in *The Pursuit of Purity*, p. 4, Dr. David O. Beale. Greenville, SC: Unusual Publications, 1986.
[2]Stott, John R.W. *God's New Society*. Downers Grove: Inter Varsity Press, 1979. p. 172.
[3]Stott, John R.W. *Involvement: Being a Responsible Christian in a Non-Christian Society*. Old Tappen: Fleming H. Revell Company, 1984. p. 61.

Chapter 2
[1]Colson, Charles. *Kingdoms in Conflict*. Grand Rapids: William Morrow/Zondervan Publishing House, 1987. pp. 268,269.
[2]Ibid., p. 27.
[3]Foster, Richard J. *Money, Sex and Power*. San Francisco: Harper and Row Publishers, 1985. p. 201.
[4]Rienecker, Fritz and Cleon Rogers. *Linguistic Key to the Greek New Testament*. Grand Rapids: Zondervan Publishing House, 1976. p. 549.
[5]Foster, p. 215.
[6]Ibid.
[7]Ibid., p. 204.
[8]Forbes, Cheryl. *The Religion of Power*. Grand Rapids: Zondervan Publishing House, 1983. p. 114.
[9]Ibid., p. 118.
[10]Ibid., p. 119.
[11]Green, Michael. *Evangelism Now and Then*. Downers Grove: Inter Varsity Press, 1979. p. 39.
[12]Foster, p. 189.
[13]Fleming, C. Kenneth. *He Humbled Himself*. Westchester: Crossway Books. p. 11.
[14]Hughes, Kent and Barbara. *Liberating Ministry from the Success Syndrome*. Wheaton: Tyndale House Publishers, Inc., 1987. p. 46.
[15]Bennis, Warren and Bart Nanus. *Leaders*. New York: Harper & Row Publishers, 1985. p. 21.

[16]Messer, E.Donald. *Images of Christian Ministry.* Nashville: Abingdon Press, 1989. p. 103.
[17]Barclay, William. *The Letters to the Philippians, Colossians, and Thessalonians.* Philadelphia: The Westminster Press, 1975. p. 35.
[18]Martin, P. Ralph. *The Epistles of Paul to the Philippians.* London: The Tyndale Press, 1959. p. 96.
[19]Reinecker, p. 550.
[20]Barclay, p. 35.
[21]Packer, J. I. *Knowing God.* Downers Grove: Inter Varsity Press, 1973. p. 54.
[22]Martin, p. 100.
[23]Vine, W.E. *An Expository Dictionary of New Testament Words.* Old Tappen: Fleming H. Revell Company, 1940.p. 139.
[24]Martin, P. Ralph. *Philippians.* Waco, Texas: Word Books Publisher, 1983. p. 87.
[25]Ibid., p. 78.
[26]Hughes, p. 47.
[27]Martin, *Philippians*, p. 87.
[28]Ibid., p. 99.
[29]Gingrich, F.Wilbur. *Shorter Lexicon of the Greek New Testament.* Chicago and London: The University of Chicago Press, 1965. p. 137.

Chapter 3
[1]Kroll, Woodrow. *The Vanishing Ministry.* Grand Rapids: Kregel Publications, 1991. p. 39.
[2]Green, Michael. *Evangelism Now and Then.* Downers Grove: Inter Varsity Press, 1979. pp. 14-15.
[3]Green, Michael. *Evangelism in the Early Church.* Grand Rapids: William B. Eerdmans Publishing Company, 1970. p. 203.
[4]Stott, John R.W. *God's New Society: The Message of Ephesians.* Downers Grove: Inter Varsity Press, 1980. p. 167.
[5]Jeremiah, David. *Escape the Coming Night.* Dallas: Word Publishing, 1990. p. 89.
[6]Barclay, William. *The Gospel of Matthew - Volume I.* Philadelphia: The Westminster Press, 1975. p. 249.
[7]Issue 40, p. 11

[8]Briscoe, D. Stuart. *Let's Get Moving.* Ventura: Regal Books, 1978. p. 17.

[9]Barackman, Floyd H. *Practical Christian Theology.* Grand Rapids: Kregel Publications, 1992. p. 17.

[10]Hull, Bill. *The Disciple Making Pastor.* Tarrytown, New York: Fleming H. Revell Company, 1988. pp. 44,45.

[11]Ibid.

[12]Guinness, Os. *Dining With The Devil.* Grand Rapids: Baker Book House, 1993. p. 24.

[13]Hull, p. 96.

[14]Barclay, pp. 140-141.

[15]Piper, John. *Desiring God.* Portland: Multnomah Press, 1986. pp. 157, 158.

[16]Ford, Leighton. *The Christian Persuader.* Minneapolis: World Wide Publications, 1966. p. 50.

[17]Stott, John R.W. *What Christ Thinks of the Church.* Grand Rapids: William B. Eerdmans Publishing Company, 1958. p. 116.

[18]Stott, John R. W. *Decisive Issues Facing Christians Today.* Old Tappan, New Jersey: Fleming H. Revell Company, 1990. p. 67.

[19]Schaeffer, Francis A. *The Complete Works of Francis A. Schaeffer: A Christian Worldview, Volume 4.* Westchester, Illinois: Crossway Books, 1982. p. 321.

Chapter 4

[1]Naisbitt, John. *Megatrends.* New York: Warner Books, 1982. p. 2,3.

[2]Barclay, William. *The Gospel of John, Vol. I.* Philadelphia: The Westminster Press, 1975. p. 26-30.

[3]Lindsell, Harold. *The New Paganism.* San Francisco: Harper and Row Publishers, 1987. p. 106.

[4]Ibid., p. 104-107.

[5]Rienecker, Fritz and Cleon Rogers. *Linguistic Key to the Green New Testament.* Grand Rapids: Zondervan Publishing House, 1976. p. 646.

[6]Naismith, James. *The Bible: The Inerrant Word of God.* Toronto: Everyday Publications Inc., 1978. p. 15-18.

[7]Hiebert, D. Edmund. *Second Timothy.* Chicago: Moody Press, 1958. p. 101.

[8]Kent, Homer A. *The Pastoral Epistles.* Chicago: Moody Press, 1958. p. 291.

[9]Barclay, William. *The Letters to Timothy, Titus and Philemon.* Philadelphia: The Westminster Press, 1975. p. 148.

Chapter 5

[1]Lundquist, Carl H. *Silent Issues in the Church.* Arlington Heights: Harvest Publications, 1984. p. 12.

[2]Rienecker, Fritz and Cleon Rogers. *Linguistic Key to the Greek New Testament.* Grand Rapids: Zondervan Publishing House, 1976. p. 655.

[3]Arndt, William F.and F.Wilbur Gingrich. *A Greek-English Lexicon of the New Testament and Other Early Christian Literature.* Chicago: The Unviersity of Chicago Press, 1957. p. 266.

[4]Tregelles, Samuel Prideaux. *Genenius' Hebrew and Chaldee Lexicon.* Grand Rapids: William B. Eerdmans Publishing Co., 1949. p. 123; Harris, R. Laird, Gleason L. Archer, Jr., and Bruce K. Waltke. *Theological Wordbook of the Old Testament,* 2 volumes. Chicago: Moody Press, 1980. p. 111; Wilson, William. *Wilson's Old Testament Word Studies.* McLean: MacDonald Publishing Co., n.d. p. 91.

[5]Kidner, Derek. *Genesis.* London: The Tyndale Press, 1967. p. 110.

[6]Rienecker, p. 474.

[7]Kent, Homer A. *A Heart Opened Wide.* Grand Rapids: Baker Book House, 1982. p. 102.

[8]Reinecker, p. 395.

[9]Tasker, R. V. G. *The Second Epistle of Paul to the Corinthians.* London: The Tyndale Press, 1958. p. 100.

[10]Schaeffer, Francis A. *The Complete Works of Francis A. Schaeffer: A Christian World View.,* 5 Volumes. Westchester: Crossway Books, 1982. p. 358.

[11]Hendriksen, William. *New Testament Commentary: Thessalonians, Timothy, Titus.* Grand Rapids: Baker Book House, 1979. p. 395.

[12]Morris, Leon. *The Epistles of Paul to the Thessalonians.* London: The Tyndale Press, 1956. p. 144.

[13]Ibid., p. 149.

[14]Rienecker, p. 612; Morris, p. 138; Hendriksen, p. 188.

[15]Morris, p. 138.

[16]Ibid., p. 144.
[17]Hendricksen, p. 199.
[18]Adams, Jay E. *Competent to Counsel.* Grand Rapids: Baker Book House, 1970. p. 44-50.
[19]Kreeft, Peter. *Making Choices.* p. 186.

Chapter 6
[1]Kaiser, Walter C. *Quest for Renewal.* Chicago: Moody Press, 1986. p. 14-15.
[2]Ibid., p. 9.
[3]Barclay, William. *The Gospel of Matthew, Volume 1.* Philadelphia: The Westminster Press, 1975. p. 197.
[4]Tasker, R.V. G. *The Gospel According to St. Matthew.* London: The Tyndale Press, 1961. p. 73.
[5]Harris, R.Laird, Gleason L. Archer, Jr., and Bruce K. Waltke. *Theological Wordbook of the Old Testament.* 2 volumes. Chicago: Moody Press, 1980. p. 1:26.
[6]Barclay, p. 99.

BIBLIOGRAPHY

Adams, Jay E. *Competent to Counsel.* Grand Rapids: Baker Book House, 1970.

Arndt, William F. and F. Wilbur Gingrich. *A Greek-English Lexicon of the New Testament and Other Early Christian Literature.* Chicago: The University of Chicago Press, 1957.

Barackman, Floyd H. *Practical Christian Theology.* Grand Rapids: Kregel Publications, 1992.

Barclay, William. *The Gospel of John, Volume I.* Philadelphia: The Westminster Press, 1975.

Barclay, William. *The Gospel of Matthew, Volume I.* Philadelphia: The Westminster Press, 1975.

Barclay, William. *The Letters to the Philippians, Colossians, and Thessalonians.* Philadelphia: The Westminster Press, 1975.

Barclay, William. *The Letters to Timothy, Titus and Philemon.* Philadelphia: The Westminster Press, 1975.

Beale, David O. *In Pursuit of Purity.* Greenville, SC: Unusual Publications, 1986.

Bennis, Warren and Burt Nanus. *Leaders.* New York: Harper & Row, Publishers, 1985.

Briscoe, D. Stuart. *Let's Get Moving.* Ventura: Regal Books, 1978.

Colson, Charles. *Kingdoms in Conflict.* Grand Rapids: William Morrow/Zondervan Publishing House, 1987.

Fleming, C. Kenneth. *He Humbled Himself.* Westchester: Crossway Books, 1989.

Forbes, Cheryl. *The Religion of Power.* Grand Rapids: Zondervan Publishing House, 1983.

Ford, Leighton. *The Christian Persuader.* Minneapolis: World Wide Publications, 1966.

Foster, Richard J. *Money, Sex and Power.* San Francisco: Harper and Row Publishers, 1985.

Gingrich, F. Wilbur. *Shorter Lexicon of the Greek New Testament.* Chicago and London: University of Chicago Press, 1965.

Green, Michael. *Evangelism in the Early Church.* Grand Rapids: William B. Eerdmans Publishing Company, 1970.

Green, Michael. *Evangelism Now and Then.* Downers Grove: Inter Varsity Press, 1979.

Guinness, Os. *Dining With The Devil.* Grand Rapids: Baker Book House, 1993.

Harris, R. Laird, Gleason L. Archer, Jr., and Bruce K. Waltke. *Theological Wordbook of the Old Testament,* 2 volumes. Chicago: Moody Press, 1980.

Hiebert, D. Edmund. *Second Timothy.* Chicago: Moody Press, 1958.

Hendriksen, William. *New Testament Commentary: Thessalonians, Timothy, Titus.* Grand Rapids: Baker Book House, 1979.

Hughes, Kent and Barbara. *Liberating Ministry from the Success Syndrome.* Wheaton: Tyndale House Publishers, Inc., 1987.

Hull, Bill. *The Disciple Making Pastor.* Tarrytown, New York: Fleming H. Revell Company, 1988.

Jeremiah, David. *Escape The Coming Night.* Dallas: Word Publishing, 1990.

Kaiser, Walter C. *Quest for Renewal.* Chicago: Moody Press, 1986.

Kent, Homer A. *A Heart Opened Wide.* Grand Rapids: Baker Book House, 1982.

Kent, Homer A. *The Pastoral Epistles.* Chicago: Moody Press, 1958.

Kidner, Derek. *Genesis.* London: The Tyndale Press, 1967.

Kroll, Woodrow. *The Vanishing Ministry.* Grand Rapids: Kregel Publications, 1991.

Lindsell, Harold. *The New POaganism.* San Francisco: Harper and Row Publishers, 1987.

Lundquist, Carl H. *Silent Issues in the Church.* Arlington Heights: Harvest Publications, 1984.

Martin, P. Ralph. *The Epistles of Paul to the Philippians.* London: The Tyndale Press, 1959.

Martin, P. Ralph. *Philippians.* Waco, Texas: Word Books, Publisher, 1983.

Messer, E. Donald. *Images of Christian Ministry.* Nashville: Abingdon Press, 1989.

Morris, Leon. *The Epistles of Paul to the Thessalonians.* London: The Tyndale Press, 1956.

Naisbitt, John. *Megatrends.* New York: Warner Books, 1982.

Naismith, James. *The Bible: The Inerrant Word of God.* Toronto: Everyday Publications Inc., 1978.

Packer, J. I. *Knowing God.* Downers Grove: Inter Varsity Press, 1973.

Piper, John. *Desiring God.* Portland: Multnomah Press, 1986.

Rienecker, Fritz and Cleon Rogers. *Linguistic Key to the Greek New Testament.* Grand Rapids: Zondervan Publishing House, 1976.

Schaeffer, Francis A. *The Complete Works of Francis A. Schaeffer: A Christian World View,* 5 volumes. Westschester: Crossway Books, 1982.

Stott, John R. W. *Decisive Issues Facing Christians Today.* Old Tappan, New Jersey: Fleming H. Revell Company, 1990.

Stott, John R. W. *God's New Society: The Message of Ephesians.* Downers Grove: Inter Varsity Press, 1980.

Stott, John R. W. *Involvement: Being a Responsible Christian in a Non-Christian Society.* Old Tappen: Fleming H. Revell Company, 1985.

Stott, John R. W. *What Christ Thinks of the Church.* Grand Rapids: William B. Eerdmans Publishing Company, 1958.

Tasker, R. V. G. *The Gospel According to St. Matthew.* London: The Tyndale Press, 1969.

Tasker, R. V. G. *The Second Epistle of Paul to the Corinthians.* London: The Tyndale Press, 1958.

Tregelles, Samuel Prideaux. *Gesenius' Hebrew and Chaldee Lexicon.* Grand Rapids: William B. Eerdmans Publishing Co., 1949.

Vine, W. E. *An Expository Dictionary of New Testament Words.* Old Tappen: Fleming H. Revell Company, 1940.

Wilson, William. *Wilson's Old Testament Word Studies.* McLean: MacDonald Publishing Co., n.d.